Timber Newsletters 2014-2017

Edgar (Ted) Stubbersfield

Copyright © 2014 Rachel Stubbersfield

All rights reserved.

ISBN: 0-9944157-8-8
ISBN-13: 978-0-9944157-8-3

Table of Contents

January 2014 Newsletter 2
   Plain talking about Plastic Decking..2
   Two Happy Customers 3
   The Holidays have not been Wasted 5
   Feedback on Hardwood Grading Guide 6
February 2014 Newsletter 7
   Different Ways to Prepare Rails...7
   Fungal Growth..8
   A "Dear Lord Give Me Strength" Moment 9
March 2014 Newsletter 10
   Hardwood at Groundline 10
   Project for Horse Lovers 11
April 2014 Newsletter...13
   Timber Queensland Flooring and Decking Seminar 13
   A Look at Wood Durability..13
   A Nice Project at Kurnell 15
   Bollards Need to be Fit for Purpose 17
May 2014 Newsletter 18
   Outdoor Structures Products now Produced by DeckMaster 18
   Advice on Deck Inspections (Guest Contributor) 18
   Decay caused by incorrect surface application 20
   LifePlus Project in Armidale 20
   Let the Buyer Beware 22
June 2014 Newsletter 23
   Guides Available from Timber Queensland...23
   Unauthorised use of OSA images on Another Website 23
   Our Image Gallery is There to Help You 24
   A reminder on Dressed Decking 24
   Springsure Truss shows why our Bridges are Different...25
   Timber - Find the Right Application for the Species 26
July 2014 Newsletter 29
   Changeover to Deckmaster 29
   Life Expectancy of Deckwood 30
   Good Detailing on Handrails..31
   Project - Capembah Creek (Myora Springs), North Stradbroke Island................................33
August 2014 Newsletter 1
   Getting Started in 3D Printing..1
   Developments at Outdoor Structures Australia..2
   More on Good Handrail Design 4

Timber Newsletters 2014-2017

- Induction Course for Timber ... 4
- Ipswich City Builds a Great Boardwalk ... 5

September 2014 Newsletter ... 8
- Plastic or Hardwood Bollards ... 8
- Laser Etching (Not a paid commercial) ... 12
- New Barrier Fence Coming ... 13

October 2014 Newsletter ... 14
- Dance Floors and Decks ... 14
- How Not to do a Handrail Post ... 16
- New Barrier Fence Here ... 18
- Be Courageous Spending your Clients Money ... 19
- OSA Decking Chosen over Plastic for Cooktown Deck ... 19

November 2014 Newsletter ... 21
- "You are a Don Quixote, Ted" ... 21
- New Deckwood Option to Help you Avoid Arguments ... 22
- Introducing the Restaurateur Decking ... 23
- Pine Posts - There is a Difference ... 23
- More on Leaving Plastic to Tupperware ... 24
- F14 Appearance Grade or F17, Which is the Best? ... 24

December 2014 Newsletter ... 26
- Why does no-one listen about 150x150? ... 26
- 150x150 An Exception ... 27
- Timber Induction Course Eligible for CPD Points ... 27
- More on Plastic Bollards ... 28

January 2015 Newsletter ... 30
- Durability of Thermally Modified Wood ... 30
- Feedback on 150x150 warning ... 31
- Timber Induction Course eligible for CPD Points ... 31
- Deck, Queen Elizabeth Drive Canberra ... 32
- Canberra Bollards ... 34

February 2015 Newsletter ... 36
- 3D Printing Explained in 60 Seconds ... 36
- 50 mm Joists - A Reminder ... 36
- Timber Induction Course eligible for CPD Points ... 37
- A Special Note for my Baptist Readers (and Historians) ... 37

March 2015 Newsletter ... 38
- Standards You Can Drive a Bus Through ... 38
- A Real Life Ghost Story ... 40
- Timber Induction Course Eligible for CPD Points ... 41

April 2015 Newsletter ... 42
- Talking Timber with Ted ... 42
- Nail or Screw Your Domestic Deck? ... 42
- Welcome to New Readers from NSW LALC ... 43
- Log Footbridge ... 44

May 2015 Newsletter 45
Where is Timber Construction Headed 45
Wisdom of High Design Loads 46
I need Help With Architectural Battens 48
June 2015 Newsletter 49
Your Opportunity to Inspect Forestry Research Centre 49
Feedback on Being Able to Drive a Bus Through Timber Standards 50
Why do I bother? 50
Paint System for External Structures (Not a paid advertisement) 51
New Book Being Written 52
July 2015 Newsletter 53
When to Use Stainless Bolts and Brackets 53
New Book Almost Complete 57
August 2015 Newsletter 58
New Publication Now Available 58
Images Sought for New Book 59
How to Ensure the Correct Verandah Joist Life 60
Forest Red Gum – Something I Just Noticed 61
September 2015 Newsletter 62
New Publication Being Finalised 62
Fence Images Sought 63
Using Laminated Beams Externally 63
Using LVL Joists Externally 65
October 2015 Newsletter 66
New Publication is Finalised 66
Bollards - Let the buyer beware 67
Fence Images Sought 69
November 2015 Newsletter 70
Ted Has Finally Found Something More Durable Than Deckwood 70
Designing for the Local Climate 71
Expert Witness 71
Some Basics about Boardwalks/Decks 72
Writers Block - It is real 73
December 2015 Newsletter 74
Same Plans - Two Different Products 74
Expert Witness 75
What does a London Bus have in Common with my Bridges? 75
Decay in Treated Pine 77
Writers Block - it is real 78
January 2016 Newsletter 80
Large Price Reduction on Deckwood 80
Timber Fence Book Finalised 80
Why so Hard to do the Right Thing??? 81
Decay in Treated Pine 82

February 2016 Newsletter 84
Report on Timber Queensland Seminar, February 25. 85
Fencing Brackets 86
.Timber Fence Book Finalised... 88
What Do You Do With a Good Idea?.. 88
March 2016 Newsletter 90
A Reminder about Sleepers 90
How to Measure End Splits 91
World's Largest Timber Structure 92
April 2016 - Special Edition 96
Large Timber Structures 96
April 2016 102
Recycled Timber - Political Correctness? 102
Large Timber Structures Followup... 105
Everything Fencing 105
May 2016 107
Coming Soon - My New Book on Timber Joints. 107
Non Durable Timber Has Lasted More Than 100 years.. 108
June 2016 115
Galvanised Bolts More Variable Than Timber 115
The State of Timber Research in Australia... 117
Published in Memento Du Forestier Tropical 118
Problems looming with self drilling screws 119
Largest Timber Church in Australia 119
July 2016 122
What Brand Paint Should I Use?... 122
More on Galvanised Bolts 123
The State of Timber Research in Australia... 124
Concrete Sleepers or Timber? 126
August 2016 128
Tamedia Building, Zurich.. 128
Revised Standard AS/NZS 1170.2 Released 128
The Two Henry Fords of Housing... 128
They Are Not Using Shipping Containers Are They?... 130
September 2016 131
Difference Between Hardwood, Pine and Cypress.. 131
Plastic Decking with Termites 132
Brief trip to the Philippines 133
October 2016 136
Coconut Wood.. 136
New WoodSolutions Design Guide for Mid-rise Developments 138
Lui the Wood Turner is a Fan of Tanacoat... 138
Full Day Timber Seminar at Broncos League Club 141
Trusses - A Brief History... 141

November 2016 145
Choosing The Correct Decking Fasteners 145
Covered Bridges and the Birth of American Engineering... 146
Width to Thickness Ratio - An Old Bridge Revisited 147
Corroding Galvanised Joist Hanger - New Guidelines 148
Three New Wood Solutions Technical Guides 149
Guest speaker at Brandon & Associates Symposium... 150

December 2016.. 151
Choosing the Correct Decking Fasteners 151
Tube Nuts - An Old Bridge Revisited 153
Largest Timber Gable Truss in Australia 155

January 2017... 158
A Dreadful Deck in Canberra is Finally Made Safe... 158
Choosing the Correct Decking Fasteners 160
Natural Images E Newsletter Released 162

February 2017... 163
Using Heart In Timber 163
Salt Storage Shed East Windsor, New Jersey, United States 166
Span Chart Software 166

March 2017.. 167
New Book On Timber Joints All But Complete 167
A Decent Garden Wall 167
How Long Will a Timber Deck Last?... 168
Stump Caps 170
Case History - RothoBlass Headquarters, Italy 170

April 2017 173
Did I See the Monstrosity in Barcaldine?... 173
How Not to Install a Post 174
Sons of Gwalia Headframe Restoration Options.. 174
I'd Give That Landing 5 out of 10 177

May 2017... 178
This Timber Library is Cyclone and Earthquake Resistant.. 178
Jack Has a Rant About Dodgy Treatment 182
When is H3 not H3?.. 183

June 2017... 184
How to Protect and Keep Your Deck Looking Good By Steven Koch (with slight tweaks by me).................. 184
Joining Decking on Commercial Decks... 187
Kim Bowman Music 189

July 2017... 190
Choosing Timber by Colour - A Lesson from Japan.. 191
City of Gold Coast Builds an Outstanding Deck.. 192
What Decking Profile is That 193

August 2017.. 194
Important Changes to Consultancy Arrangements... 194

It Seemed a Good Idea at the Time	195
Something Else That Seemed a Good Idea	195
A Wood Encouragement Policy - A Mixed Blessing?	197
Mareeba Shire Turns to Timber Bridges over Concrete	199
September 2017	201
Be Careful with Ply Fencing	201
Wood Encouragement Policy. What is needed	202
Cairns Regional Council Sets the Standard for Preservation	204
October 2017	206
Writing a Book on External Furniture	206
Is Recycled Timber Seasoned?	207
New Book for Those Interested in Plywood	208
Be Careful Choosing Your Species	209
November 2017	210
Should Decks be Load Limited?	210
It's a Good Idea to Pre-oil Your Decks	210
The Customer Isn't Always Right	211
Timber Garden Retaining Walls	212
Writing a Book on External Furniture	212
December 2017	214
Another Deck Collapse	214
How to Confirm the Correct Treatment Has Been Achieved	214
The Importance of Grading Timber	215
Lessons from a 30-year-old mangrove boardwalk	216
About the Author	219

2014

January 2014 Newsletter

Plain Talking about Plastic Decking
Two Happy Customers
Holidays have not been Wasted
Industry Feedback on Hardwood Grading Guide
Index to Newsletters

Plain talking about Plastic Decking

I was contacted recently by an engineer who advised me that he is going to specify Deckwood as a replacement for a plastic composite deck that had failed. Next issue I hope to have the images, (cropped so as not to identify the location) which show the present state of the deck that is only about six years old. I simply cannot comprehend why people are coming to the conclusion that using this type of material is an advance over using correctly detailed, correctly supplied and correctly installed hardwood. It all comes down to doing your homework and checking what you are told and being very skeptical. Take this chart below as an example of the information available on composite decking.

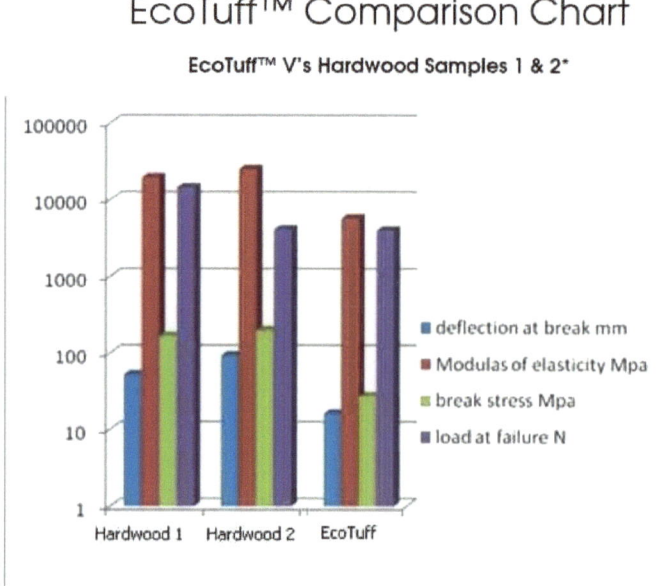

When we were doing our research on plastic decking one company said that they had a product ideal for our needs and sent through comparative test results of our product against theirs (Deckwood is Hardwood 1 and LifePlus is Hardwood 2 in the bar chart above). I had to stop and think as this showed a very good comparison of this particular plastic decking against hardwood which I knew from everybody else's figures could not be right. Then I had another look, the scale is logarithmic, there is the same distance between 1 and 10 as there is between 10 and 100 as there is between 100 and 1000!!. If you want a true visual comparison look at the following graph showing a 3 point bending test showing LifePlus (at top), Deckwood, (second top) and three common brands of plastic below.

We found one product that did impress us. It was not because this composite decking would carry the commercial load but because the company owner was extremely honest about the shortcomings of his products and had excellent design support but only for domestic applications. He had a similar philosophy to me. He said straight out, this product is not suitable for commercial applications. Sadly I see this product now advertised by a reseller for commercial applications.

We can understand a specifier wanting to have a replacement for timber but imagining a perfect replacement product in your mind does not make it a

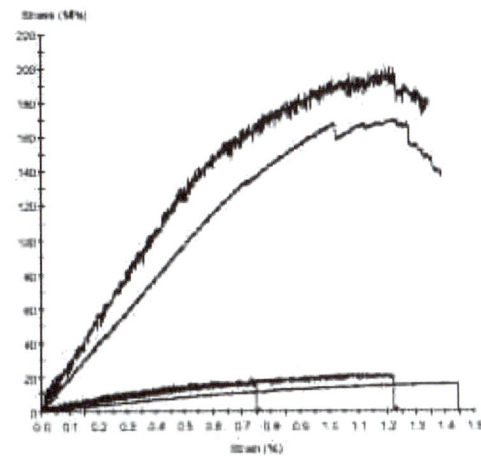

reality. (Now we are going a bit deep as it sounds like the Ontological Argument for God's existence and this is not a newsletter on philosophy). In your commercial applications you have to apply the same rigour to plastic decking as you should be applying to timber. You have to be able to say that it will carry a 4.5 KN and 5 KPA load. You have to be able to say that no board will deflect beyond a serviceable limit when fully loaded. Ask yourself, "What will happen if someone rides a horse on this deck" - and yes it has happened and yes, the horse went through it? If you are contemplating plastic decking contact us and we will tell you what questions you have to ask.

If you missed it, There is a discussion on decking alternatives by Ralph Bailey of Guymer Bailey Architects in the march 2013 Newsletter. The June 2011 Newsletter deals with boardwalks and fire.

Two Happy Customers

We prepared this fence for a council in NSW. We guarantee that it will not rust despite being coastal and because the posts are installed according to our instructions it will age gracefully. The client said "We are really happy with the product and result. You are welcome to use these photos in promotional material if suitable".

It differs from our standard 3 rail fence in that the rails are ex 150x50 instead of 175x50, there is a custom spacing and the spotted gum timber is dressed after treating. The tops of all the rails are rounded to shed water which is standard.

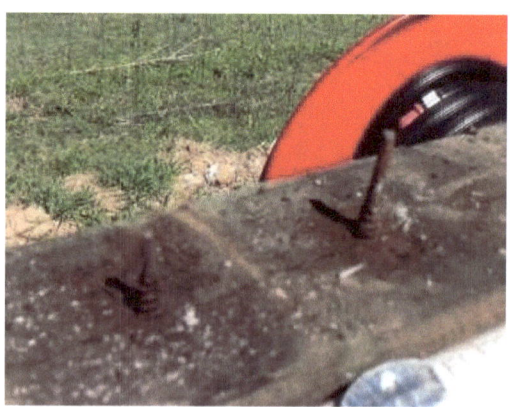

Unfortunately there isn't a before and after picture here to show the staggering transformation. My old friend, Ray Ferdinand, (in a different life quite an accomplished builder and former Mayor of Gatton) came to me to supply replacement decking for a pool in the hills outside of Gatton. The material is 145x45 Deckwood. He was delighted with the finished result. If you are not convinced about Deckwood by now you never will be, what is important to notice here are the joists and the screws. The 50 mm joists are split from end to end which has to happen as the screws cannot be staggered. The 75mm joists were also split as the screws in these also were in a straight line. Remember never to use 50mm joists with 14# screws. Ten years of drought was the only thing that saved these timbers. The screws on the original deck were badly corroded - perhaps they had the yellow zinc finish, maybe they were galvanised but I doubt it. Remember - within 8-10 K of the sea it HAS to be stainless and for other applications it is not worth the price difference using galvanised. Read my Timber Preservation Guide for the reasons.

The Holidays have not been Wasted

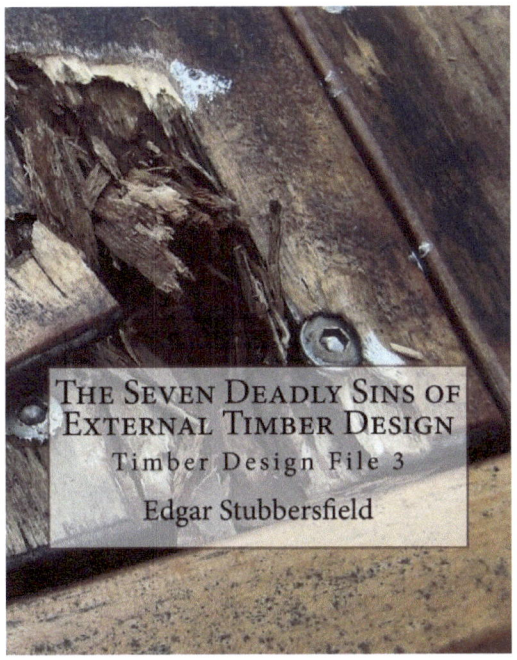
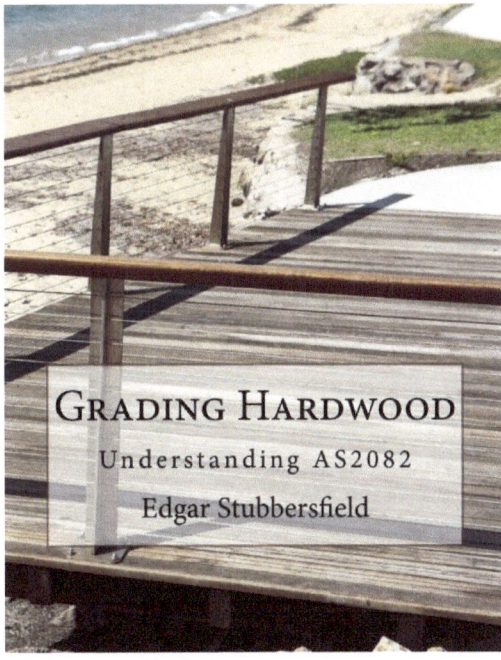
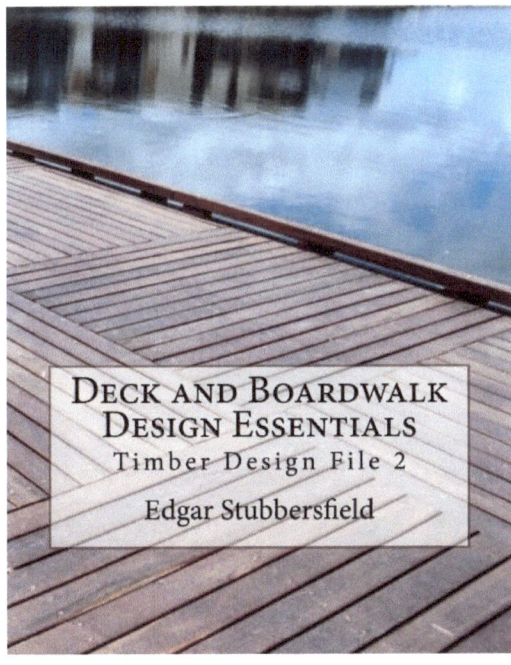

Over the break I reformatted four of my Timber Design File books and published them on Amazon. They are not as pretty as the treatment guide and one day I hope I will have them redone professionally but they look a lot better even though the text is the same. You can still purchase the PDF from me but if you want a hard copy you can order them from Amazon, Barnes and Noble, and Book Depositary.

The timber newsletters are a bit expensive as a hard copy ($60 US) but there are 250 pages, most with multiple colour images but you can still download the unformatted contents for free from my website and purchase the PDF for $33.

Feedback on Hardwood Grading Guide

If you have ever written a specification that says F14 or F17 you need to understand what it means. I will guarantee it does not mean what you think it means. If in doubt, read the feedback on the latest guide from Bill Thorne, Wholesale Manager at Parkside Timbers.

Ted,
We both thought that it was just what we need in an industry that is fast losing it most experienced people, with the current trends of more "one shop " building supply centres, the lack of timber knowledge in the staff is becoming a real problem as they are unable to give good advice on timber as they have not been properly trained. Your grading book should at least give them a working knowledge of what is required. I can see it becoming a standard tool for most places to have so that their staff have a recognised industry standard to which they can refer for the basic knowledge needed.

February 2014 Newsletter

Different Ways to Prepare Rails
Visible Fungal Growth
A "Give Me Strength Moment"

Different Ways to Prepare Rails

The two images above show three ways a timber traffic barrier rail can be processed. The rails in the top image show two versions of our 190x44 Continuous Rail. The rail on the left shows one of our rails that was treated with Tanalith E to H3 and then dressed. The rail on the right was dressed then treated with Tanalith E. The second rail has a uniform brown colour from the preservative. The timber rail in the lower image looks untreated and has not been dressed. It is not as pleasing to the eye as either of the rails above refer to last month's newsletter for an image of a whole fence with the dressed after treating option. Now there is not a big difference in the timber specification but there are differences, it is not dressed for a start and we use better species as well.

 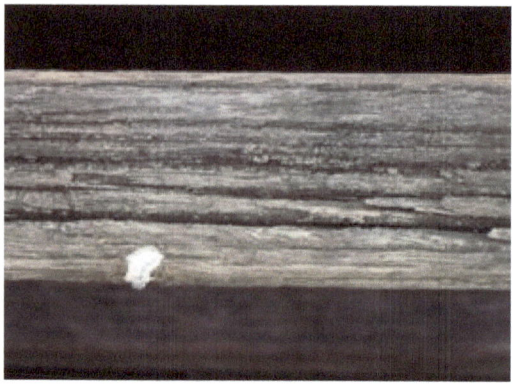

One thing we noticed is the need to shed moisture on these rails even though they only have a small top surface area. The rail on the right is a 20 year old piece from one of my bridges. I thought, I could do better and after taking that image always ensured that the tops of our rails had a radiused top surface. Not enough years have gone by to tell you it is a great success but it should perform better.

So, with your rails you can continue in your old ways our you could specify 190x44 Continuous Rail by Outdoor Structures or its licensees in either treated after dressing finish or dressed after treating finish. The standard lengths are 3.6 m and 2.7 m. Other sizes are available. Talk to us about your needs.

Fungal Growth

 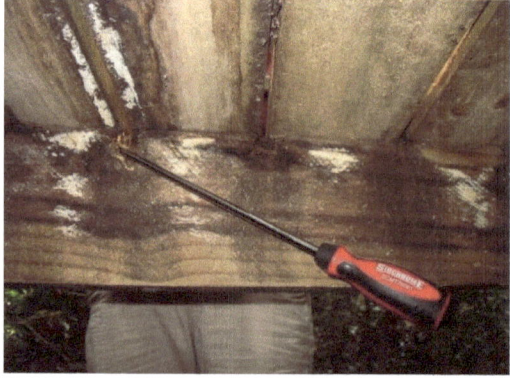

In the October 2012 newsletter I gave a summary of the coroner's report on the deck fatality at Yeppoon where a young baby died. There, the builder who was called in to inspect the deck did not understand the significance of fruiting bodies that could be seen on the underside of the decking. Fruit bodies of decay fungi are often leathery-looking brackets or they can look like mushrooms and the colour ranges from white to brown. Spores are released from gills or pores. You would think that it would be easy to spot and identify something so obvious.

These two images from a recent consultancy (used with permission) show examples of where it is not so clear. When looking at the white flecks, you cannot tell if we are looking at patches of vegetative fungal growth; (not spore-forming) or a flat fruit body (reproductive structure; spore forming). When you see the presence of this type of material on the outside of timber you should to test the affected areas to see if it is just something on the surface or a symptom of internal decay. On the image on the left the decay was clearly evident once I started trying to push the spike into the treated pine brace. The brace has exposed end grain which allowed moisture to enter which then caused it to decay. Once the decay started, it then spread into the joist to which it is bolted. The added lesson here is don't clutter your design and avoid exposing end grain, especially in pine.

A "Dear Lord Give Me Strength" Moment

Some time ago, when I was interviewing someone for a job in sales, I told him that people who work for me tend to become very religious. "What do you mean?" he said. I explained that people will do things that are so exasperating that it will not be too long before I hear you say, "Dear Lord, give me strength". Let me tell you of a recent "give me strength moment"

We supplied some of our decking to a job and sometime after we had a call back from the client that we forgot to dress the face of the decking. To assist us, and without making a call to chastise us, they ran it through a planer and reduced the thickness by 5 mm. Immediately the timber is probably undersize for the load but more importantly they lost the slip resistance provided by the rough sawn face. When we had it tested, freshly Tanacoated Deckwood went R12 but if decking had a dressed face it was highly likely that someone would slip. Unless you have a roof over you should not be considering dressed faced decking.

Edgar Stubbersfield

March 2014 Newsletter

Hardwood at Groundline
Writing Blog for Timber+DESIGN Magazine
A Project for Horse Lovers
Index to Newsletters

Hardwood at Groundline

I was out driving with my wife on Sunday when I noticed this fence that has fallen over. It is no more than 10 years old, probably less. The posts are hardwood and of course they are set into concrete which then decayed at groundline and simply snapped off. The posts are hardwood but that does not mean much if the lowest priced tenderer did not pay extra for the better performing timber. But at the end of the day purchasing the better hardwood will not prevent, just delay the inevitable. Hardwood and concrete do not mix, It makes no difference if sawn timber is treated or otherwise. How do you do it correctly? Follow this link See also the March 2011 Newsletter. Knowing how to put a post in the ground is not "secret men's business" but is basic knowledge every tradesmen is paid to know.

But what about treated natural rounds? Years ago I was at a conference on power poles and one of the speakers addressing the subject of ground line maintenance said that one of the worst areas for ground line decay was in the Lockyer Valley - i.e. the poles I was supplying were performing poorly. Why hadn't anyone said anything to me - because they met specification. At that conference we were told that the answer was going to be a shrink wrapped bandage full of preservative. Prior to that the pole was excavated to a depth of about 450 mm and creosote poured in and mixed with the backfill. I am now told that the bandage actually promoted decay because the pole could not breath

Ground line maintenance is still being conducted and these two images show it being done to a pole outside of our premises. This happens every five years and the shrink wrap bandage has now been replaced with a loose fitting bandage with boron pellets. Strangely, it appears that the wrap is not installed when the pole first goes in the ground before any decay has taken place.

How effective is this maintenance? It really isn't known what the service life of a power pole actually is. It is thought to be 40 years. The difficulty is that a powerline is generally upgraded and the poles replaced with larger ones before they have to be removed due to failure. This mucks up any statistics. Groundline maintenance is amplified upon in my Timber Preservation Guide.

So, even if you have been careful and not used concrete you still need to maintain a H5 CCA pole at ground line. There is a lot to be said for upgrading critical poles that will not be maintained to H6 but then, with pigment emulsified creosote you do not want to be touching them.

Project for Horse Lovers

A projects that Chris completed late last year was to supply material and assembled doors for a stable built in Gatton. This stable block is built within a more or less standard kit metal shed. The rails on the stalls were 125x50 spotted gum and the slats were 88x19 spotted gum decking. The walls were downgrade life plus, by downgrade, I mean to our standards. I particularly like spotted gum for horse and cattle yard rails as it is unlikely to shatter if an animal hits it hard. This resilience is why spotted gum is recommended for handles in striking tools.

When we produced decking we pulled out all the short lengths (under 1.8m) which meant that we ended up with a large quantity of shorts that we did not know what to do with. Then every so often a job comes along that requires a lot of shorts such as a ramp. Do your timber supplier a favour. If you need 200 pieces at 1.2m don't order 50/4.8m, he might even let you have them at a discount.

April 2014 Newsletter

Timber Queensland Flooring and Decking Seminar
A Look at Wood Durability (Guest Contributor)
A Nice Project at Kurnell
Bollards Must be Fit for Purpose

Timber Queensland Flooring and Decking Seminar

On April 1, the ABC aired a timely reminder on substandard decks, sadly it was no April Fool's Joke. How serious is this problem? Archicentre have recently issued a press release saying that in their opinion there are probably 12,000 life threatening decks in the country, now that is not dodgy decks, but decks that have the potential to kill. Their press release 10 years ago gave the figure at "only" 8000, this is a 50% increase. Has there been a 50% increase in the number of decks over 10 years or has the incidence got worse. I put that question to Ian Agnew of Archicentre Brisbane. Hopefully we will have the answer for next month

On the same day as the ABC feature, Timber Queensland held a seminar in Brisbane on flooring and decking where about 250 people heard excellent presentations on how to design decks well by Colin Mackenzie and Ralph Bailey.

For more reading on deck collapses look at earlier newsletters Deck Collapses - February 2010
Coroner's Report Released on Deck Fatality at Yeppoon – October 2012
Yet another Deck Collapse - March 2013

I was talking to one of the delegates about our LifePlus and Deckwood products and he commented "Now all I have to find is a client prepared to pay the extra". My response was that. "All you have to find is a client who won't sue you if goes wrong" To emphasise this point a presentation on litigation against builders was given by Craig Sawford, CBP Lawyers. It should have driven complacency from all attending but I am afraid I am pessimistic on such matters.

A Look at Wood Durability

This article has been contributed by Jack Norton who formerly headed up the timber preservation section of the DPI. Jack is well known in the Queensland Timber Industry and has been a friend of many years. When not masquerading as a mild mannered public servant he was known as Kaptain

Edgar Stubbersfield

Preservation. Now in retirement he provides expertise on timber treatment processes and chemicals, advice on durability, development of specifications and standards, product quality assessments and training. **His warning about using durability levels from overseas sources is extremely important.** *Contact me for his address*

Once timber is put into service, it is exposed to attack by a insects and decay (or rot). These biological hazards can be controlled by design and detailing, the use of naturally durable wood or preservative treatment. In this article, we will look at natural wood durability and how knowledge of the durability of a species influences how the timber might be used.

All commonly used species of timber have two major zones; sapwood and heartwood. The sapwood is the outer band that carries water and nutrients up and down the stem.

In the heartwood, the fluid pathways that once carried water and nutrients are filled with resins, extractives, waxes and other materials and it is these resins and extractives etc that give a species its resistance to attack by insects and decay. (Ted Here - see the images in the July 2013 newsletter)

Intuitively, most people will know that if hoop pine and ironbark are put in the ground, the hoop pine will decay (or rot) before the ironbark. The ironbark is said to be more durable than hoop pine.

Australian Standard AS5604 *Timber – Natural durability ratings* defines 'natural durability' as "the inherent resistance of a timber species to decay or to insect or marine borer attack". This standard classifies 360 species of timber according to the following classification (Table 1)

Table 1 Natural durability classification in Australia		
Class	Probable in-ground life expectancy (years)	Probable above-ground life expectancy (years)
1	More than 25	More than 40
2	15 to 25	15 to 40
3	5 to 15	7 to 15
4	0 to 5	0 to 7

It is important to note that natural durability ratings apply to material from heartwood only. The sapwood of all species of timber is deemed to be non-durable and needs to be impregnated with wood preservative chemicals to increase its durability. Heartwood can not be effectively protected/impregnated by wood preservative chemicals and so you can not change its natural durability.

Another point worth noting is that the classifications shown in Table 1 are decay related classifications. As far as durability against insects and termites are concerned, a species is either resistant or not resistant. This information is also presented in AS5604. Engineers and building specifiers use these natural durability ratings when designing structures.

It is hard to compare Australian durability ratings with those used by other countries. Examination of the information in Table 2 shows that durable timbers (class 1 and class 2) are expected to perform a lot longer in Australia than in other countries. As a result, care should be used in applying durability classifications from overseas to construction specifications in Australia.

Class	1	2	3	4	5
	Probable life in years				
Aus A'Gnd	> 40	15 to 40	7 to 15	0 to 7	
Aus I'Gnd	> 25	15 to 25	5 to 15	0 to 5	
EU	> 5	3 to 5	2 to 3	1.2 to 2	< 1.2
China	> 9	6 to 8	2 to 5	< 2	
Japan	> 9	7 to 8.5	5 to 6.5	3 to 4.5	< 2.5
Malaysia	> 10	5 to 10	2 to 5	< 2	
Bangladesh	> 3	2 to 3	1 to 2	< 1	
Tanzania	> 10	5 to 10	2 to 5	1 to 2	< 1
Brazil	> 8	5 to 8	2 to 5	< 2	
USA	????????				

A Nice Project at Kurnell

Credits
Asset Owner: Sutherland Shire Council
Design: Sutherland Shire Council
Construction: Cooper Constructions
Timber: Deckwood and Joistwood

A project does not have to be large to be pleasing. This small deck at Silver Beach, Kurnell is a good example. It was built on the foreshore at Kurnell using our Deckwood and Joistwood. One of the unusual aspects to this is that the client required that the timber be inspected for grade by an independent grader. There should be more of this. More to the point, the council had the wisdom to ensure that it was being grading to an appropriate standard. Of course, we can help with both determining what that grade should be and with grading.

For more details on this project contact Blake Spurrier, *Cooper Construction Services*, Unit A4, 13-15 Forrester Street, Kingsgrove, NSW 2208. t: 02 9502 2586 f: 02 9502 2686 m 0422 408 581 M: 0422 408 581

To reinforce the importance of grading see
Identify and Assess that defect May 2012
Case History showing Unsuitable Decking Sept 2013

Bollards Need to be Fit for Purpose

The ABC news on the 7th April also showed footage of an accident where a car crashed through a bollard into the foyer of a new public building. Several people were injured. There is a perception that if you put a point on a piece of timber it was a bollard but as my Guide to Bollards, Traffic Control and Fencing establishes that different applications need different products. In the video below you can see a policeman carrying away what was an attractive but hollow bollard that has sheered off during the accident.

http://www.abc.net.au/news/2014-04-07/several-injured-after-car-crashes-into-gold-coast-hospital/5372194

Bollards are not as simple as you may think. Talk to us, we will help you come up with a bollard that is buildable, durable and fit for purpose.

Edgar Stubbersfield

May 2014 Newsletter

Outdoor Structures now Available from DeckMaster
Advice on Inspecting Decks (Guest Contributor)
Decay Caused by Incorrect Surface Application
LifePlus Project in Armidale
Let the Buyer Beware

Outdoor Structures Products now Produced by DeckMaster

Chris Blackledge has been manufacturing my product range under the name of Infrastruction Pty Ltd since June 2012. The products will now be produced by DeckMaster, situated in Ipswich, Queensland. Chris Blackledge and I have joined forces with Deckmaster. Chris will be in a primary sales role and myself retained to help with timber design consultation etc.

The same phone numbers have be retained and Chris and I will still be available to you. This will allow our Outdoor Structures product lines to be available to a greater audience through DeckMaster's nationwide network of Distributors.

Advice on Deck Inspections (Guest Contributor)

In last month's newsletter I commented on the latest Archicentre press release about the number of life threatening decks in the country which had increased from approx. 8,000 ten years ago to approx. 12,000 now. I asked whether the number of decks has increased by 50% or have standards dropped even further.

When speaking with Ian Agnew of the Brisbane office of Archicentre, he advised that the situation with decks is so serious that they are advocating regular inspections similar to those required for pool fencing. I wholeheartedly agree. Archicentre have kindly contributed the following article on how to inspect decks. Note that this is not just a timber problem but relates to all decks regardless of material. - over to Archicentre.

"Balcony or deck collapses during recent years caused by bad building practice or poor maintenance have caused serious injury and in some cases resulted in tragic deaths.

Elevated balconies and decks – whether constructed of timber, steel or concrete – are exposed to the extremes of climate and need to be periodically checked for deterioration because of the risk they can pose for residents and visitors. Homeowners and tenants should check their deck annually for rotting timbers, shaky hand rails, loose balustrades, corroded fittings, rust stains or cracking and seek professional advice if necessary.

The following information is not meant to replace a professional assessment by a qualified person such as an architect or engineer, but it does provide an indication of what to beware of:

Timber Decks

- Identify the species of timber and make sure it is suitable for external use. Oregon, for example, may not be appropriate for external structures. It is distinguishable by a broad softwood grain pattern and by a pinkish colour when fresh surfaces are exposed, for instance where timber has split.
- Check for any compression or deformation of the structural members.
- Test the timber by probing it with a sharp object like a screwdriver. Decayed timber will feel soft and spongy.
- Check connection points at the beams with a screwdriver for deterioration as timber can rot at junctions.
- Make sure the timber balcony is properly fixed to the main house structure, for instance, using bolts or where timber framing extends into the house structure.
- Check the base of timber posts for rot and check brackets and bolts for signs of rust.
- Posts need to be securely anchored into the ground and not just bolted into paving.
- Check handrails and balustrades to make sure they are not rotted or unstable.

Concrete Balconies

- Look for signs of deflection. If the balcony slopes away noticeably away from the building, there may be a problem.
- Examine the underside of the concrete balcony. Rust stains or exposed steel reinforcement are signs of a serious problem.
- Check handrails and balustrades to make sure they are not loose or unstable.
- The presence of spalling, where chunks of concrete are crumbling off, may be a serious problem and indicates the need for inspection by an expert immediately.

If you're unsure, get some advice from an independent professional and restrict the use of the deck or balcony until you can be sure it's safe."

Decay caused by incorrect surface application

LifePlus, our domestic decking is a very trouble free decking system. Follow the guide (after you have purchased it for only $22), don't deviate and it will reward you with a deck that will age gracefully. ***LifePlus*** is made primarily from spotted gum but even spotted gum is not immune from early decay when you do the wrong thing. This dressed face spotted gum domestic decking illustrated is only three years old yet it has decayed. The reason here is that it has received several coats of a film forming finish all round and the timber cannot breath and the trapped moisture has allowed it to decay. The owner should have applied a high quality penetrating oil such as our ***Tanacoat***. The decay at the end grain is compounded by the builder cutting the end of the decking square instead of back bevelling to ensure that moisture is not trapped.

The other reason you would not use a film finish is because it is simply too slippery when wet.

LifePlus Project in Armidale

Builder: Dan Murray, Red Constructions, Tamworth NSW 0401 387 240

A recent very happy customer in Armidale sent me these images of a deck on his own home that he built with our patented LifePlus. Because LifePlus is used on private residential work I do not get the same opportunity to take images so I was very grateful. When I developed LifePlus it was intended for fully weather exposed applications but it works even better under a roof.

This decking is fastened from underneath to a rail attached to the joist. It is a very neat finish. the decking is coated with Tanacoat. When specifying LifePlus you should use the words *"LifePlus Decking installed in accordance with the LifePlus Decking Guide".* That way is someone puts it down with a nailing gun you have the right to demand that it be ripped up and start again.

Let the Buyer Beware

This week I had two distressed pensioners come to my office. They had purchased 160 m of decking at an online auction site and, on taking it home considered it unusable. They could not afford to take the financial loss they thought was involved. Over half of the 160 m were short at approx. 1.2 m long and they thought also of poor quality. Much of the balance in longer material they also thought was unusable too. It was purchased as "feature grade decking". They were right.

The Australian Standard grade descriptions for decking allow select, medium feature and high feature. While I don't think the last two should ever be used for decking they are defined standards and conformance to grade is easy to assess. On inspection, a large portion of the batch did not meet the very generous allowance of high feature grade. The Auctioneers told the pensioners 'tough luck" but changed their tune after a visit to consumer affairs and an offer of a certificate from me of non compliance to the advertised description. The manufacturer was trying to pass of firewood as decking.

The lesson: Be very careful when purchasing decking at an auction and steer clear if it is described as feature grade. If the price seems too good to be true it probably is.

June 2014 Newsletter

Guides now Available from Timber Queensland
Unauthorised use of OSA images on Another Site
Our Image Gallery is there to help You
A Reminder about Dressed Decking
Springsure Truss Shows why our Bridges are Different
Timber - Find the Right Application for the Species

Guides Available from Timber Queensland

 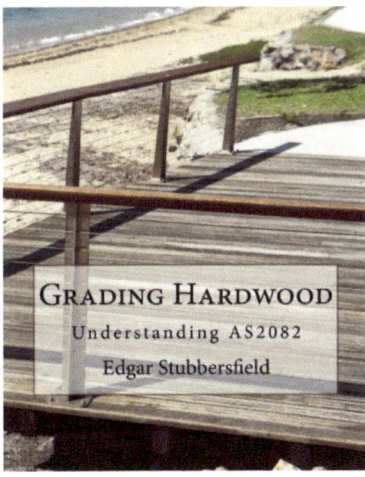 

Up till now, if you had wanted a hard copy of my guides, as opposed to the PDF, you would have had to purchase them from Amazon, Barnes and Noble, and Book Depositary, then wait up to three weeks for them to arrive. My younger readers seem to prefer PDF's but we older ones still want to have a book in our hands. Fortunately, relief is at hand. Timber Queensland has just started to stock three of my books. This will save you a lot of time. To order the books visit Timber Queensland's Online Shop and they will be shipped to you within 24 hours.

Unauthorised use of OSA images on Another Website

Some of the best images of our products are not to be found on my website! We had found Recycled Timber NSW (A division of Ironwood Taree Pty Ltd.) had six of our projects up on their website and passed of as theirs. A letter from the photographer's solicitor saw that taken down but no payment was made to the photographer despite it being requested. If you want to see some more of our products visit Ironwood Australia's website and look through their Recycled Australian Hardwood Bollards page and scroll through their images. When I visited the site on June 18 they were all my images taken by Dennis Clarke Photography and none were of recycled hardwood. In fact there are not far short of 30 of my images on that site including two on the lead in page to their products section.

Our Image Gallery is There to Help You.

Getting the right image for a report can always be a problem. My website has a very large image gallery which is there to help you (but not my competitors). Have you discovered it yet. Here is the link. They are sorted into the different categories and then into different projects within that category. Select a project that seems interesting and click on that hyperlink. You will find a series of thumbnails and often information about the project. Find an image you need in the thumbnails and double click and a higher resolution image pops up which can be saved. Need an even higher resolution image, contact us.

What do you do with it then. You are free to use it providing you acknowledge copyright. Some of it is held by my wife and some by a Dennis Clark Photography. The agreed wording is Copyright Outdoor Structures Australia, used with permission.

A reminder on Dressed Decking

One of my first consultancies was to look at a large public deck built by a developer as part of the council requirements. Some years after construction I was called in to look at it as there were problems and it needed certification. All our design information had been ignored. The decking was dressed face spotted gum. I advised that the deck could not be certified as it could not meet the slip resistance required under the disability code. Recently a pendulum tester was baught in to check my advice. The decking failed miserably, as it had to, though a higher reading would have been achieved if they had tested using the inclined ramp method but still not high enough.

I know dressed face decking looks prettier but it is dangerous. When I tested 145x45 Deckwood with a coating of Tanacoat it went R12.

Springsure Truss shows why our Bridges are Different

Thin steel damaged by mower

Thin steel needs stiffener to attach braces

When you purchase footbridges you must remember that they can and do fail. The truss bridge that failed during the Maccabiah Games in Israel is infamous. This just doesn't happen overseas. A few months ago I saw a trussed bridge in Australia that had also collapsed. The deck portion just dropped into the creek! It was not an old bridge either! The fact that it had an engineer's certificate would have been of little comfort to anyone that could have been hurt.

The recently supplied 22 metre OSA Design Warren Truss that was delivered to Springsure is a good example of why the OSA bridge is a wise choice. The two smaller images underneath the images of our truss being installed show portions of trusses from two different manufacturers. They illustrate how light the steel in a kit truss bridge can be. In one, the council mower had buckled and put a large hole in the bottom cord. In the other the steel has to be reinforced to allow the webs to be welded in place. The steel in an OSA truss starts at 4 mm and is usually heavier. This all equates to longer life and better vibration characteristics

The paint used in the truss is PPG's PSX700, not powdercoating. Because the truss is a one piece welded frame (which is why it doesn't shake) it is too large to fit in the galvanising bath so we use a hi-tech paint system equal to galvanising. It is brilliant. Graffiti wipes off. This product is a spinoff of the space industry, PSX700 was developed to paint the steel at Cape Canaveral that has to take not only salt air and the 5000 degree flames of a a shuttle launch. The deck of course is Deckwood and the handrails are a robust custom designed system, not pool fencing which is unsuitable for footbridges.

Never purchase your bridge on price but always on specification, The links below help you write an appropriate specification and assess the bridge offered. Follow them closely and you avoid the common pitfalls with kit bridges.

Timber - Find the Right Application for the Species

Back in 1970, when I was a young man of 19, I spent three months on a rubber estate in Ceylon (as everybody still called it back then). It was a great life at the top if you didn't weaken. The culinary delights of Sri Lanka in my humble opinion are not surpassed anywhere in the world. The words, string hoppers, egg hoppers, dhal, curd and jaggery, Maldive fish and saffron rice still bring visions of delight to my mind. But one day the discussion strayed from what was on the table to the table itself. The superintendant thought it was quite funny, and so did all his friends at the planters association. It was made from rubber wood. At that time, when the rubber tree became uneconomic it was simply ripped out by the roots by an elephant and burnt. It wasn't valued and there was little infrastructure to mill the timber. There were still pit saws in operation

But the superintendant was before his time. The strength properties of rubberwood are similar to radiata pine so you could build a house with it, but furniture was what rubber wood was ideally suited for. Ikea and the likes could not survive without this low priced and large resource. Having a resource led to an industry that capitalised on that resource's properties.

These are my bookcases, the frames are made from rose gum and the shelves are brush box. Now rose gum shrinks more than the better hardwoods (over 7% officially, ours seemed to be more) and was only Durability 3 in ground so it was unsuitable as a green off saw product for many applications. When we were milling it was usually cut into roof battens installed the next day and never seen again. The timber shrunk and held the roofing screw more firmly. But who uses timber roof battens these days? But now if you go to Harvey Norman furniture shops you are likely to see furniture made from it. It is a perfect match of species to application

Brush box (almost 10% shrinkage) is unstable when it dries and so has to have the stickers that separate each layer during drying placed very close together. Despite it being Durability 3 there was a time when it was used for decking because in one of the Queensland Forestry Department's Technical Pamphlets it said you could be used that way. It was a disaster. Despite it easily reaching F17 you would not want to build anything from it. It does, however, after drying with care, excel as a decorative timber. It is excellent in solid and laminate flooring as it is so hard that high heels do not mark it

The weakness of the Australian timber and specification industry is that there is little effort to match the resource and the grade of that recourse to structural applications. Under a roof and hidden by plasterboard you can get away with a lot, but frequently you can't when exposed to view internally. Sins of omission are never forgiven when used externally. If you are still specifying your external timbers by F grades only you need to have a serious talk to us. Timber is a wonderful product but strength (i.e. the F rating) is only one consideration, and probably not the most important.

July 2014 Newsletter

Changeover to Deckmaster
Life Expectancy of Deckwood
Good Detailing on Handrails
Myora Springs - A Remarkably Well Built Boardwalk

Changeover to Deckmaster

New faces at Outdoor Structures - Left to right Tammy, Nigel and Nick framed by OSA bollards

I would like to say that the changeover from Infrastruction to DeckMaster/Outdoor Structures Australia was trouble free but to be honest there were a few bumps along the way, caused in part by the large number of orders that came in. Nigel Shaw, The owner of Deckmaster has taken steps to rectify the teething problems and has moved staff around and employed extra employees to produce the orders. Already they are looking at bigger premises. While I am still quoting and assisting customers, let me introduce the faces that will increasingly be the contacts you will be dealing with.

Nigel Shaw. I am the director and founder of DeckMaster Australia which is the new owner of Outdoor Structures Australia. I have 20 years experience in the timber industry, formerly the owner of a furniture manufacturing business. For the past 12 years I have been the managing director of Wilson Timbers and in 2011 I started another business DeckMaster Australia.

DeckMaster is a specialist wholesale decking manufacturer of concealed fixed residential decking. DeckMaster is now the new owner of Outdoor Structures Australia and I am very excited to incorporate my passion for design and timber. I am looking forward to expressing my creative side and continuing to develop the Outdoor Structures range of product with the help and consultation of Ted Stubberfield. We aim to provide excellent quality and service.

Nick Horan: Hi, I'm Nick Horan. I am part of the Outdoor Structures sales team, and enjoy working towards business development.Previously i have completed a bachelors degree in Urban Design and Planning, and have worked asan intern at Gold Coast City Council in planning and development.

I like working for Outdoor Structures Australia because I deal daily with a wide range of stakeholders to achieve projects that are high quality and extremely durable. If you would like to contact me for sales and other information I am your man! Contact me at Sales@outdoorstructures.com

Tammy Crawford: I am a bright young lady who is part of the Outdoor Structures sales team. I have 4 years experience in the timber industry working for Wilson Timbers in internal sales. I am looking forward to learning the Outdoor Structures product range and getting to know the customers. For any information or sales enquires please do not hesitate to contact me.

Life Expectancy of Deckwood

How long can you expect to receive from a Deckwood deck in full sun? If we look at AS 5604 Timber - Natural durability ratings we are told greater than 40 years but as I re-read the Standard a pink pig just flew past my eyes. That standard does not differentiate between a painted or unpainted finish and whether it is horizontal or vertical or even what part of Australia it is located. So what can you really hope for?

The Timberlife prediction software, a very useful design tool, does not cover decking. One of the researchers of that software advised me to use 20 to 25 years. It is also our experience. A longer life expectancy of 40 years (in Brisbane with Dur 1 timber) is given in Wood Solutions Timber Service Life Design. But this refers to replacement caused by decay (Refer to Table 5.4 and Figure 5.6 on pages 36). What generally happens is that durable hardwood decking is not replaced because of decay but because of physical degrade of the top surface.

A good example of this is the small bridge illustrated above which was one of the first I ever built way back in 1985. That is 29 years ago. It is in a park opposite my home and so I have been watching its performance over all this time. The deck planks were ex 200x38. Two and half years ago the deck was quite happy carrying a horse and at that time only one board had been replaced over the intervening 26-27 years. The deck did look as if it needed to be replaced because of surface degrade though appearances and actual performance were different. In recent days it was eventually replaced. So in summary, I say 20-25 years (with just a few boards replaced) is what you would expect in Queensland. Invariably those boards that need replacement will be evident in the first six months.

Good Detailing on Handrails

Back in 2005 I was walking along the Thames embankment near the London Eye when I spotted some handrail that was being replaced. It was originally installed in 1953 for the Queen's coronation. So that is a service life of 52 years. The original handrail had a very neat splice and was being replaced in the same way (illustrated). This held moisture and it eventually decayed at the splice. Beyond the splice the timber was fine. I realised then that the acceptable service life for a piece of timber is 5 to 10 years longer than you actually achieved. The image on the right above is the handrail at the Port of Cairns Authority marina. It is probably the best handrail I have seen and it is not one of mine! The rail itself has a good slope on it to shed moisture and equally important there is a significant gap between each piece so no moisture is held at the join and a finger trap is avoided. Fastening is from underneath. A small centre support is enough to hold the rail from taking a set either up or down,

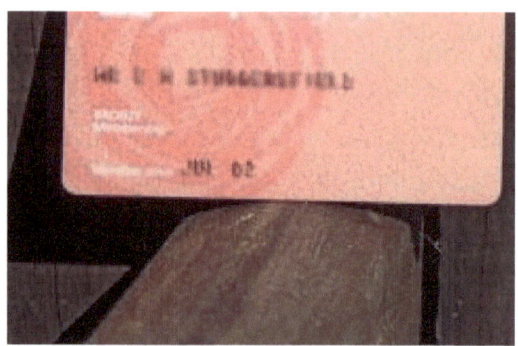

As I mentioned earlier, I had been watching the bridge opposite my house closely over the years and I noticed that the 50 mm wide handrail eventually started to show signs of degrade. The image above on the left is typical but some areas had more degrade. (The rails were actually replaced last week but I would have just rolled them over). This led me to change the design of all our handrails so that they all shed moisture. You will see this in my Commercial Barrier Guide (only $22).

Of course, the most effective water shedding handrail is when the top rail is mounted as a diamond. The image on the left is from a heritage listed cricket ground at the Gatton university. The fence is older than me and I am 63. Some rails had failed but most are still sound. We are now adding a diamond top fence to our range of commercial fencing options. They will have a dressed after treating finish. There are two options, one using a 125x125 post with a 100x100 rail and a 75x50 mid rail and the second with a 100x100 post with a 75x75 top trail and a 100x50 mid rail. The product can be customised to suit your needs.

As for the need for fastening from underneath, this image illustrates clearly its shortcomings. The main part of the handrail is fastened from underneath but then and is in good order. An extension was added and top fixed. It has failed. It is not hard to fix from underneath and well worth the extra effort.

Project - Capembah Creek (Myora Springs), North Stradbroke Island

Credits
Asset Owner: Redland City Council
Built & Project Managed by: Partnership between Quandamooka Yoolooburrabee Aboriginal Corporation & SEQ Catchments Limited.
Engineering: Peter McKay, Crighton Engineering
Construction: Tim Powell, Pacific Palms Constructions

My first Deckwood project was in a lookout in a rainforest at Mt Tamborine which was built by Tim Powell, then with the Qld National Parks. Since that time Tim (on your right in the top picture) has been a good supporter of our products and has become a friend. We supplied the boardwalk at Myora Springs to Tim about a year ago. This is a very well built structure which follows our recommendations and has close attention to detail such as designing where the joins are made and having a kerb above the deck and at a height not to trap wheelchairs.

Capembah Creek (commonly referred to as Myora Springs), , not far from Dunwich Point on North Stradbroke Island is part of the native title claim of the Quandamooka Yoolooburrabee Aboriginal Corporation and is in a culturally significant site with middens on both sides of the creek. Unfortunately the sandy creekbed had been contaminated by a large amount of road gravel washed out from the road nearby. This had to be removed and erosion stabilised with Elcorock bags.

The main piles were installed by jetting. To do this Tim fitted two pipes down the side of pile with a manifold at the top which connected to a fire pump. He drilled 900 mm and dropped the post in and backfilled. The pump was then started and two men with a spirit level guided the pile down the 3.5m required. The surrounding soil around the pile was compacted by a vibrator.

The image at the top left shows the joists going down. Note the double joist arrangement where the joins go. Note also the joists are widely spaced to maximise the spanning potential of the 145x45 Deckwood. The inner joists are lapped so the last screws are a long distance from the end so splitting at the end does not occur and the board at the end of the joist become loose. You can force a 14# batten screw into the hardwood joist without predrilling but it always splits the joist. Tim predrilled to the full depth of the screw and placed them in a staggered alignment and so avoided any splitting. Remarkably there was no splitting at the end - see top right hand image. The lower image shows that after sealing the ends with CN emulsion the ends of the protruding joists were capped. Fasteners are of course stainless.

All in all this is a remarkable job. Congratulations Tim.

August 2014 Newsletter

Getting Started on 3D Printing (Guest Contributor)
More on Good Detailing on Handrails
Induction Course on Timber
Ipswich City Builds a Great Boardwalk

Getting Started in 3D Printing

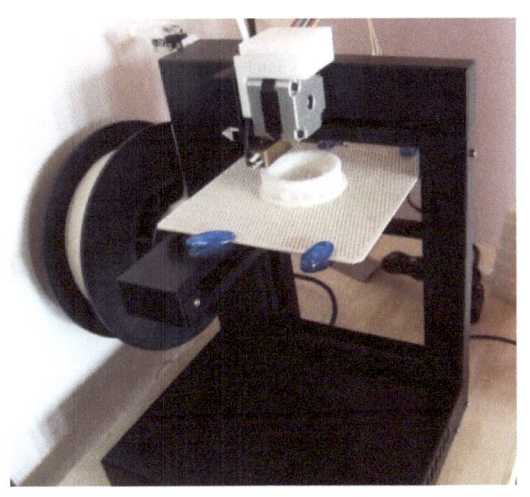

Figure 1: A basic fused deposition modeller

Figure 2 Forest Table by WertelOberfell

This article is contributed by Dr. Jennifer Loy, Program Leader Industrial Design, Convenor 3D Design Digital Media, QCA & Griffith School of Engineering, Gold Coast campus, Griffith University. QLD, 4222 Australia. With the expiration of patents and the availability now of free software, 3D printing is becoming less costly and will eventually become an everyday reality for my younger readers. For images of 3D printed bollard tops refer to the ??? newsletter

We hear in the news about 3D Printing, we are even seeing desktop 3D printers appearing in shops such as Office Works and on Amazon, but how to get started?

The first thing to know is that the term 3D printing, or additive manufacturing, refers to a range of technologies suitable for different materials and different applications. The most basic ones are called Fused Deposition Modellers. These are essentially filaments of material heated and extruded to build up a shape, rather like using a glue gun. *Figure 1: shows basic fused deposition modellers using a single filament of ABS plastic*

These range in price from approx. $2,000 up to approx. $70,000 depending on build size, number of print heads and the materials used. Designing for printing on these machines can be frustrating to start with, as you need to understand how to design to reduce the necessity for support scaffolding in the build, but a good tip is to design objects that grow rather like a tree and so do not require much in the way of support structures (*see figure 2 Forest Table by WertelOberfell*). If you are new to 3D computer modelling, you can try it out using free software, such as Google Sketch Up 3D, Autodesk 123 or TinkerCAD. They take a bit of getting used to, but are good to practice on. It is also possible to generate models using photographs of an object you have made in clay or wood with Autodesk 123, though these facilities are more for fun than anything work related.

If you are thinking about printing in metal, then you need, realistically, to have at least a million dollars in your pocket. Although this is the area that has seen the most dramatic developments in the last few years, it is also very challenging. Working with titanium powder can be dangerous as it is volatile and also needs argon gas in the build chamber to keep in under control. This is a heath hazard and heath and safety nightmare.

My recommendation for anyone thinking about working with 3D Printing is to attend a short course – libraries, and facilities such as The Edge in Brisbane, run day courses in 3D Printing, and to visit an online service provider such as Shapeways or iMaterialise for further information. This will give you an insight into the types of objects you can print and inspiration for what you can do. Happy Printing!

Developments at Outdoor Structures Australia

Expansion of Premises: Nigel Shaw, the CEO has signed the documents to lease a much larger premises in Ipswich to allow for the expansion of the business.

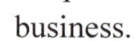

Purchase of a CNC Router: A CNC router with a bed size of 4.2x1.2m has been purchased. This is going to allow us to manufacture bollards with your, or your project's logo. Signage should be straight forward as well.

New Range of Shelter Sheds: We have been granted the rights to manufacture a very attractive shelter designed by Peter Shepherd of Continium Landscapes__- thank you Peter. It is available in a 2.7 and 3.6m long version. It will not be too long before we have images of installed products.

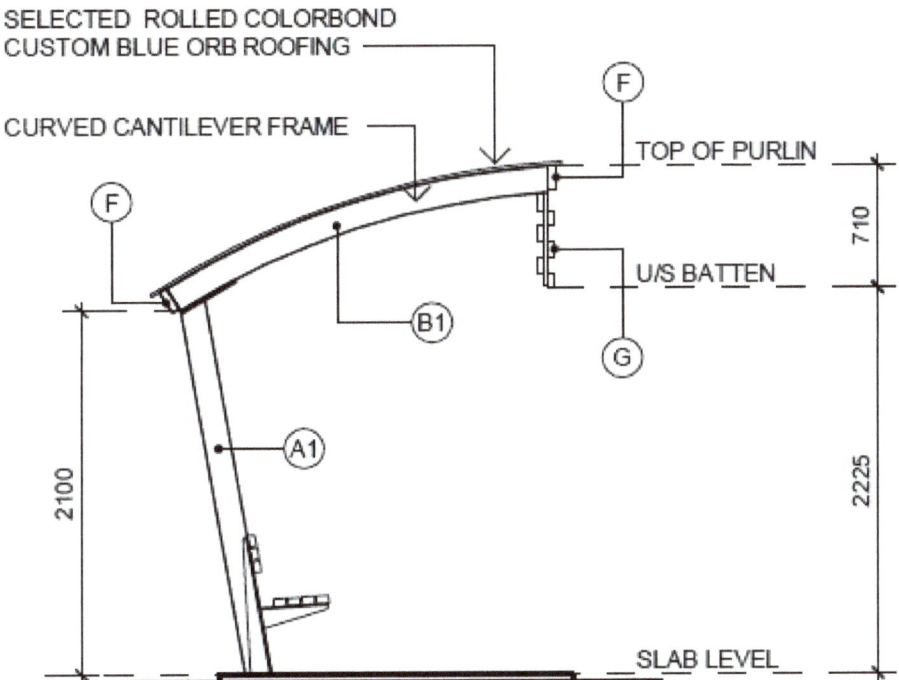

OSA Constructions: Installation was always my weak point. We had and still do work with some really great companies and had/have no hesitation in recommending them. They were more set up for the larger jobs though. Nigel has started a new company OSA Constructions which can give an installation price.

New Sales Representative: Nigel has appointed Keith Smith to represent Outdoor Structures Australia. Keith is an experienced business development professional, with over 20 years of sales and marketing experience, having held senior sales and management positions across a diverse range of industries. He joins OSA from Waco Kwikform, a multi-national organisation providing scaffolding and formwork solutions to major building and construction projects. Keith has previously operated his own business as an independent supplier and consultant to the building industry.

More on Good Handrail Design

Last month I wrote on how to design handrail for maximum durability and aesthetics. I included an image from the Cairns marina showing a handrail which I said represented the very best in handrail design. Unfortunately my image could have been better as the details were not clear. My friends at Ports North kindly sent a better one to share with you. Note, sloping top, gap between rails, fastening from underneath and centre supports. Stainless posts are great (but so is durable hardwood).

Our Commercial Barrier Guide will help you with handrail design.

Induction Course for Timber

Recently I was asked whether I could deliver an Induction seminar on the use of timber, particularly weather exposed hardwood. I was wondering whether there is a demand for such a program on a wider sphere. I would appreciate feedback from my readers on firstly, whether there is a demand and secondly what subjects need to be addressed. Additional consultants can be bought in to deal with subjects outside of my area of expertise. Topics could include but not be limited to:

Timber Preservation.
Hardwood Grading.
Timber Decks – Designing for Durability,
Utilising Small Diameter Hardwood.
The Seven Deadly Sins of Timber Design.

Ipswich City Builds a Great Boardwalk

Nigel Shaw CEO of Deckmaster (Left) with Ken Swan (right) and Paul Ploetz from Ipswich City Council of the Open Space Construction Team, Ipswich City Council

Nigel Shaw, CEO of Deckmaster and I recently visited a boardwalk we supplied to the Pan Pacific Peace Gardens in Redbank, Queensland. We met with Mark Mathewson, Coordinator of Infrastructure Services, Open Space Construction Team and Ken Swan and Paul Ploetz who made it happen. Ken and I have spoken often and he brought to the project a detailed understanding of building for durability and a passion for doing it well.

The Pan Pacific Peace Gardens, started in 1992, was constructed to commemorate soldiers who camped on that site before embarking to fight in the Pacific during to of World War II. "Inspired by Ipswich's history, the Pan Pacific Peace Gardens feature memorial plantings, formalised pathways and boardwalks that wind through extensive wetlands. The gardens also act as a wildlife corridor linking Redbank Rifl e Range with adjoining lands and rivers". Initially this project was a "gift" by a power distribution company and appears its implementation was budget driven as sadly it embodies poor timber design and supply and as a consequence the timber bridges and boardwalks are not faring well. I can understand but not excuse a resistance to using timber.

One boardwalk, passing through the Bernard Treloar Rainforest Collection had to be replaced. Being in a shaded area this boardwalk should have lasted for a very long time but it was thought to be only 12 or years old when replaced. I must stress, if you are not prepared to do exposed timber well don't do it at all. This time the design of the replacement and construction of the new boardwalk was carried out in house by Ipswich City Council. This boardwalk uses 120x35 Deckwood and 150x75 Joistwood. It follows our design and construction guides closely The result is superb and is a credit to Ipswich City Council and its employees.

Fortunately the old concrete foundations were still in excellent condition. A layer of Bayer's Kordon anti termite barrier was inserted between the foundation and the timber sole plate. At the end they terminated in concrete with the foundations integrated with approach path. This avoids trip hazards. The design ensured that there is at least 300 mm of clearance between the joists and the ground.

While the shade from the trees protects from UV, when building in these situations it is especially important to have self cleaning decks. The patented Deckwood profile allows leaf litter to drop

through. Equally important is to lift the kerb up off the deck. The spacer is 75mm to ensure the footplate of a wheel chair does not clash. Changes of direction are done through fan tapers. Our standard tapers go from 60 to 90 .mm. All the timber was coated all round with CN oil and the cut ends were sealed with CN Emulsion.

All in all, a very commendable job

Edgar Stubbersfield

September 2014 Newsletter

Plastic or Hardwood Bollards
Laser Etching for Signage
New fencing System

Plastic or Hardwood Bollards

Broken plastic bollard and Intact hardwood traffic barriers in a park opposite my home

The first order of traffic barriers I ever supplied, way back in 1984, (for the mathematically challenged that is 30 years ago) was installed in a park directly opposite my home. See comments in the July 2014 newsletter under handrail design. They have only ever received two coats of oil in all that time and normally nothing is ever done to them. There was a large amount of material involved yet there have been minimal replacements. I would advise the council to budget for replacement in about 20 years time. Can you really hope for better service?

You can imagine my surprise when new bollards that are being installed in the same park are made from plastic. Well it is a modern product so it has to be better, right, as one manufacturer says they are "long lasting and require less maintenance than traditional materials". But it is not so simple. Quite frankly I think I could break them off at ground level if I tried and already some of them have broken. Feedback from customers has told how whole rows of them have been broken off by the bullbars on 4 wheel drives. Try doing that with one of my bollards! It is far from clear that plastic product lasts longer and will require less maintenance.

So am I saying wood is better in every application? It does not follow. Take this bollard on the right which is meant to take a vehicle impact. When this streetscape was being developed I had a deputation of three employees from that council and the designer. They wanted to know how to make it a success as replacements were going to be very difficult. It was simple enough:

- Use Durability 1 in ground timber
- Form expansion joints along the length
- Cap the top
- Set in no fines concrete

Now I would probably say add a pole bandage as well in this specific application. The drawings were duly prepared and not one piece of advice was adopted. I later sold them caps but that will not stop the premature decay in the ground. Steel, with tar epoxy at the base and concrete filled would have been better than timber used contrary to best practice. Plastic of course would be a non starter.

Why does plastic even get a look in? And this I am afraid lies solely with the timber industry that have been their own worst enemies and dare I say landscapers who have looked to maximise profits at the expense of quality.

Material supplied by others when OSA was specified

These four images clearly show why plastic is making inroads. Compared to these low quality and low price timber barriers and bollards, plastic is a better option. These examples were not a case of poor specification as our product had been asked for. The difficulty is getting some contractors to realise that a specification actually means something. Invariably our main customers are local and state government as they are not looking to maximise profit, they want trouble free items. Trouble free items will always be dearer than a landscaping sleeper with a slope on the top.

But compared to a well supplied and installed hardwood bollard, plastic will always be a poor second choice. But what about pine?

So called treated pine

The difficulty with pine is getting material that is truly treated to H4. The image above and to the left shows the cross section of a pine bollard where the timber has been treated with a die to show the treatment. There is a large portion in the centre which is very clearly untreated. It can never be treated with conventional processes as the heart of pine is just as untreatable as the heart of hardwood. The second image on the right shows how this untreated section decays leaving the treated sapwood on the outside.

This can be countered by the process of incising (see image to the left) but I do not know anyone in Queensland doing it. Incising forms slits along the length of the piece that fill with chemical thus protecting the heart. When incising you have to ensure that it is done to a depth of 10 mm. The piece shown was from a trailer load of incised timber I purchased but found it was only done to a depth of 3 mm. I had to virtually give it all away in the end as it would not pass registration under the Timber Utilisation and Marketing Act here in Queensland at the time. It was an act of gross stupidity to get rid of this Act now anything goes in the timber industry from some suppliers. I suppose that is another argument for plastic! The pine rails also are far more easily broken than hardwood.

If there is one final argument against plastic it has to be that they look dreadful. Take these spotted gum customised eclipse bollards we are preparing for a customer. The client wanted something that will make his shopping centre stand out from the rest and he will certainly have that. The spotted gum is dressed and has two coats of Tanacoat.

So, if you are thinking of plastic think of Joan Rivers who died recent. She had said of her plastic surgery that when she died she would send her body to Tupperware. You could not say it was a good look. You can colour plastic as much as you want to try and look like timber but it is still plastic and can never have the beauty you are seeking. Leave plastic to Tupperware and be more careful in how you purchase your timber.

Laser Etching (Not a paid commercial)

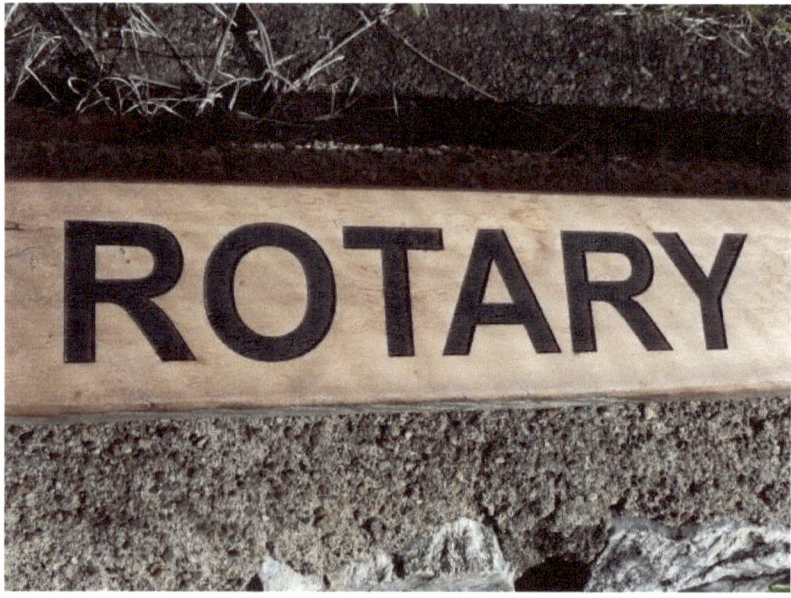

A client recently obtained a sample of unoiled spotted gum to experiment with laser etching a sign for a seat he was purchasing. I was aware of laser cutting of timber but living in country the etching process had passed me by. I think the result is very impressive and of course it can be done on a variety of materials, not just timber. This particular sign was done by Laws Laser in Geebung (Ph 3865 3244). This would be very good in conjunction with our traffic barrier rails.

New Barrier Fence Coming

Over the years I have had a good friendship with Mr Kurata of Kurata Co., Ltd in Japan as well as his Australian representative Claus Jehne. On his last visit to Australia Mr Kurata showed me images of a fence he made for the Nihon Daira Zoo near Shizuoka (not far from Mt Fuji). I realised that we had profiles similar that would allow us to produce an Australian fence inspired by this fence. I would never have thought of producing a full oval version of the Cruiserline rail and mounting it sideways.

We intend to make available our Australian fence in 1, 2, 3 and 4 rail options. If you have any interest, contact me or Keith Smith. There will be more next month.

Edgar Stubbersfield

October 2014 Newsletter

Dance Floors and Decks
How Not to do a Handrail Post
New Fencing System
Be Courageous Spending your Clients Money
OSA Decking Chosen over Plastic for Cooktown Deck

Dance Floors and Decks

Cloudland ballroom c.1950 image courtesy of State Library of Queensland

Dressed copy of my decking   Slip resistance test

I know I am showing my age but, I can remember a time when women danced with men and you actually held each other. You actually moved around a dance floor instead of standing in one place. I never got to Cloudland but I did my time at country dance halls and loved the gypsy tap. The most popular halls were the ones with the fastest floors, always improved by the liberal application of Pops (sawdust soaked in kerosene and linseed oil and then dried). "Moved" is not the right word, with leather soles on the bare boards you would glide above the surface. Litigation following injuries on "sped up" floors saw many fine floors coated with polyurethane.

How do you make a good dance floor? You start with a log of a species with naturals oils such as spotted gum or tallow wood or crows ash and then cut over thickness boards grading them to ensure they were of the very best quality. You would carefully dry the boards and then machine them with so they were thicker than normal and ensuring the tongue was offset low to enable you to sand the floor many times over its life.

How do you make a verandah board? It is the same as making a dance floor except you don't use crows ash as it is too expensive. The boards are standard size and the edges are square. The top is exactly the same as cloudland ballroom except for the gaps. Now you can get away with that under a roof where it stays dry. Somewhere along the line someone thought it was a good idea to take a dance floor, move it outside into the weather, speed it up with water and then allow frail boned grandmothers free access to it. It was grossly irresponsible. A designer could be expected not to know this but not a sawmiller. All of us, when we produced flooring or decking in spotted gum, would strap it tight with steel bands and then tie it on the truck with ropes to deliver it. You would pray that there weren't any steep hills as the boards would slip backwards out of the packs. (webbing straps put an end to that). A producer did not have to know about disability codes and slip resistance or do tests with a pendulum tester, if he stopped to think his experience told him it was dangerous. I did made the connection one day and stopped supplying dressed face boards in the weather opting only for a natural sawn finish.

We recently looked at a job where my whole decking system had been adopted even down to copying the profile of Deckwood but they made one change, they produced the decking with a dressed face. Deckwood (and LifePlus) is not just a shape, though that is part of it, neither is Deckwood (and LifePlus) a comprehensive system of building weather exposed decks An important part of Deckwood (and LifePlus) is the integrity to take you by the hand and say "Don't do this". One small change is enough to keep up the solicitors payments on the BMW for a long time. Please talk to us if you want to change something and we can talk you through the consequences.

How Not to do a Handrail Post

Not one thing about this post is right

This image shows why in the end I gave up and left the battle to younger men like Nigel Shaw, CEO of Outdoor Structures Australia. Consider the six failures in this item.

1. Timber Quality. The post has a large loose gum vein that has opened up along the length. This is a piece that should have been specified as exposed grade and in that grade not one millimetre of loose gum vein is permitted. In an F17 structural grade the permitted amount is 1/6th of the length. This post would have started as a 1.5m so even then it should only be a maximum of 250 mm long. I imagine I, and other reputable suppliers, priced this job and went to the builder with a price of say $30 per metre for in grade material. The builder would have taken one look and said, "You are too dear, I can purchase this for $25 per m". It is a good deal for the miller as this piece should have gone down the chipper. Inspections for conformance to grade should be done more often. (Incidentally I can do this now I am a free agent).

2. Builder's care. Had the builder simply taken this piece and turned it 180 degrees and placed the split outwards, the visual effect would have been far different. He may not have understood what he was looking at, i.e. what an open gum vein is and it would not have looked like this when installed, but pride in what you are building tells you that it will look a lot better if you place it away from view. It got so bad that I had to start putting labels on reversible products stating what side had to be placed away from view as I could not trust people to look at two sides.

3. Top Fixing. The screws fixing the rail to the post are just driven through the rail into the end grain of the post. Bad practice will always beat you. Moisture works its way down the screw holes and it just has to deteriorate. The only way to fasten a rail sitting on top of a post is with brackets from underneath. The image on the right is from a boardwalk where the long run of handrail is fastened the way I recommend. Then one day someone added an approach handrail and just fastened it from the top. It did not work. I covered good detailing on handrails in the July 2014 newsletter.

4. Handrail is flat. By not allowing the top surface to shed moisture the timber deteriorates far more quickly. Either sloping the rail or using one of our moisture shedding profiles would significantly improve the life of the rail without increasing the cost. Again this is covered in the July 2014 newsletter but there is a better picture in the August edition.

5. Termination of wires. Frequently we see on the drawings some lines with an arrow saying "stainless wire rope" perhaps a size and a spacing but generally a specification that you can drive a bus through. This image is a good example of why firm direction has to be given. We built a bridge for a client to their drawings which terminated in eyed coachscrews as illustrated above. the post split and we were asked to fix it. We thought it was a design fault but we held our peace and fixed it. We later were asked to build another bridge with the same detail and so we asked for the detail to be changed. They would not and the post again split. We were asked again to fix it but this time refused to do it for free. Of course we never got another job from that company.

On my website I have an AutoCAD block which you can save to your computer and just drop in your drawings where everything is detailed

6. Film Forming Finish. You can see that moisture is getting under the film at the join. This is going to promote degrade at the end grain, check out the images in the May 2014 newsletter. Also when the film breaks down, and it does not take long in our high UV, you have to sand the coating off before you can apply a new coat. We recommend Tanacoat, a penetrating oil with water repellents and UV blockers.

There is not one thing here that is difficult and could not have been fixed on paper - including confirmation grading as part of the specification. I would have also added the use of a volute washer so the handrail would not have needed retightening. Talk to us next time you are designing in timber. We can help you turn the ordinary into the extraordinary with our knowledge of detailing and specialised products. There is a book below on commercial barriers.

New Barrier Fence Here

The dimensions of the Australian version of the fence built by our friends at Kurata Co., Ltd_in Japan for the Nihon Daira Zoo near Shizuoka have been settled upon. They are summarised below in the drawing below. If you have any interest contact me or Keith Smith.

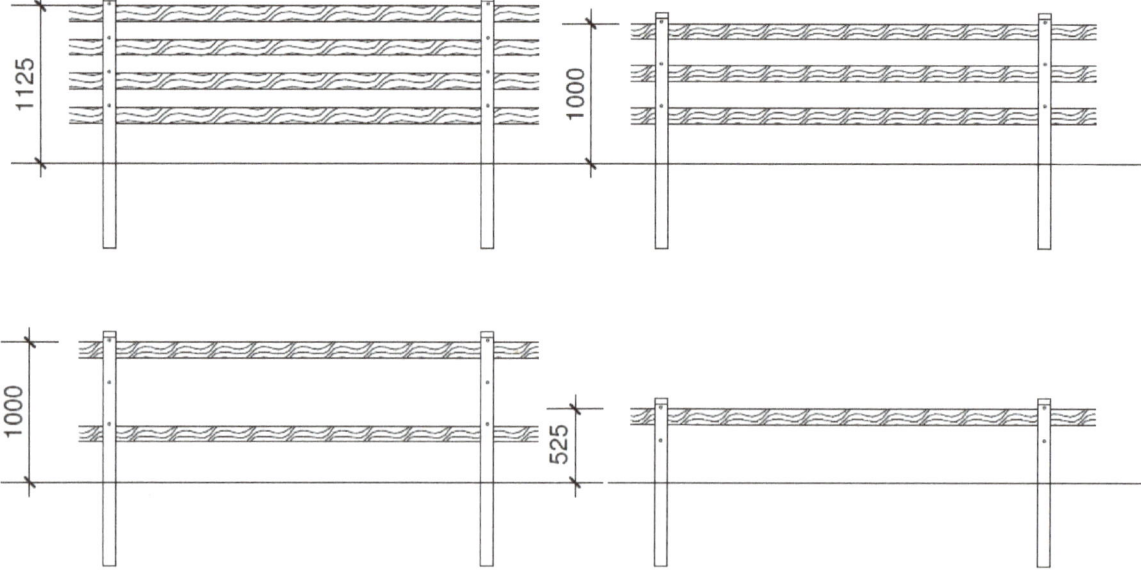

Be Courageous Spending your Clients Money

Over the years that we were supplying spotted gum to Japan I never ceased to be amazed at the creativity of the Japanese architects and the fearless attitude they took to spending their clients money. As I am approaching old age I am hit with the wisdom of the saying that old age is not for the fainthearted. To the young Architects and Landscape Architects out there reading this, don't wait till you get to be my age to be courageous. Spend your client's money courageously because if you get results like these below he/she will thank you. We will thank you if you spend it with us!!

While it seems pretty obvious that the Japanese designers did not give (at time) much thought about code compliance, or at least our codes, the look is good.

OSA Decking Chosen over Plastic for Cooktown Deck

Replacement Deck Sovereign Hotel, Cooktown

Credits
Client: Sovereign Resort Developments Pty Ltd
Design: MMP Architects, Cairns
Construction: MTC builders, Cooktown
Lifeplus Decking: Outdoor Structures Australia

Long lasting decks are very hard to build in the tropics and it was not surprising that the original deck which was only 15 years old and built from treated pine had to be replaced. While the timber was still generally intact it had become very distorted (twisted and bent) and was looking very 'tired'. During the construction of a replacement deck the opportunity was taken to make the deck larger and of a different shape.

The architect, Peter Pierce of MMP Architects initially looked at plastic decking but rejected it due to its lack of strength, poor appearance compared to timber, serious question marks over durability, and cost etc. Peter said of the OSA deck that "It's looking great. The contractor did a fantastic job, particularly in regard to compliance with your recommendations for fixing etc.". Most importantly the client is very happy with the result.

Contact Peter Pierce of MMP Architects for more information about this project and the successful use of OSA timber decking on other projects in the tropics.

Timber Newsletters 2014-2017

November 2014 Newsletter

You are a Don Quixote Ted
New Deckwood Option to Help you Avoid Arguments
Introducing the Restaurateur Decking
Pine Posts - There is a Difference
More on Leaving Plastic to Tupperware
F14 Appearance or F17, Which is Better?

"You are a Don Quixote, Ted"

I was talking recently to my friend Jack Norton, the timber preservation guru, and he said of my newsletters that I am still a Don Quixote. "Yes I know Jack," I replied, "Getting old and silly". While he did not deny that he said that what he really meant was that I was "tilting at windmills". That is of course a reference to Miguel de Cervantes' (1547-1616), work **Don Quixote de la Mancha**. The expression has many meanings but these days it frequently means taking on an opponent you know you cannot beat. I fear that my cause of the love of timber and excellence in its external use is generally a lost cause. For those out there who share the vision, let us continue to tilt at windmills.

Incidentally, if you are having a problem with timber treatment, Jack is your man. Contact me for details

New Deckwood Option to Help you Avoid Arguments

It has become necessary to add more steps to the production of Deckwood to protect specifiers. A few months back I visited a site where yet again the builder had substituted a different timber decking for the nominated Deckwood. The Architect had done a perfect job of specification but the builder, presumably wanting to maximise his profit, purchased a generic decking. It had a dressed face and was installed in an area where there was going to be a lot of water. This is a recipe for injury and litigation. I do not know the outcome but I felt very sorry for the architect who did the right thing and has to sort this mess out before someone is hurt. This is why I tilt at windmills, It is not the litigation though that is stressful enough but it is the human suffering that goes before. I have seen enough pain in those around me and I will try hard to avoid it happening to others.

We are now introducing 120x35 Deckwood Plus. It starts off as the same Deckwood that you know and all the technical information is still the same but we have introduced two changes to make it harder to copy and make non conformance even easier to identify. These are:

- The top surface is lightly brushed to remove any small "hairs" and
- The decking is preoiled all round with Tanacoat

This option only adds an extra 65 cents plus GST per metre to the product and is good value. So if this is the way you want to go, and I can't imagine why you would choose anything else, we suggest that you now specify "120x35 Deckwood Plus by Outdoor Structures Australia 07 54624255". The 120x35 Deckwood is the one that is stocked but other sizes can be made to order.

Introducing the Restaurateur Decking

Nigel is introducing a new size, 110x25, to the patented decking range and is giving it the name Restaurateur Decking. It is the decking illustrated above in the centre between 88x21 LifePlus and 120x35 Deckwood Plus. As the name suggests it is intended for commercial spaces such as restaurants. Like LifePlus, It is a kiln dried product and still uses 10# screws and 50 mm joists. Sample boards of the three deckings can be manufactured and sent to your office. Phone 07 54624255.

Pine Posts - There is a Difference

22 year old pine posts failing at groundline

If you had asked me before a recent consultation I would have said unequivocally that CCA treated pine posts were one of the success stories of the timber preservation industry. I have never had any problems but obviously this client has. Again it is a case of using the wrong product in the wrong place. The posts were only 125 mm in diameter which means they were H4 (in ground non structural) rather than H5 (in ground structural). To go from a H4 to a H5 application is a 60% increase in chemical content. These posts really did not have a chance of succeeding.

When we built boardwalks we normally used 150 mm H5 posts. Now, we were purchasing the posts so we could control whether we purchased H5 or H4 (This size is available in both treatments) and furthermore we purchased from a supplier that certified there was the required amount of sapwood in relation to heartwood (minimum of 20 mm sapwood band). So I suppose it is no surprise either that ours worked. The correct sapwood content is very important. There was a time when CCA treated peeler cores from ply mills entered the market. They looked for all intents and purposes like Koppers logs but having no sapwood could only be coloured and so failed quickly. Having your 150 mm post certified as to having the correct amount of sapwood is very good and requiring a certificate to the effect should be part of your documentation.

There is a lot to be said for bypassing 150 mm altogether as you do not know what treatment you have once you cut or bury the stamped end. At least with 200 mm it is only available in H5. I may not have gone totally silly in my old age but I am getting a lot more cynical.

More on Leaving Plastic to Tupperware

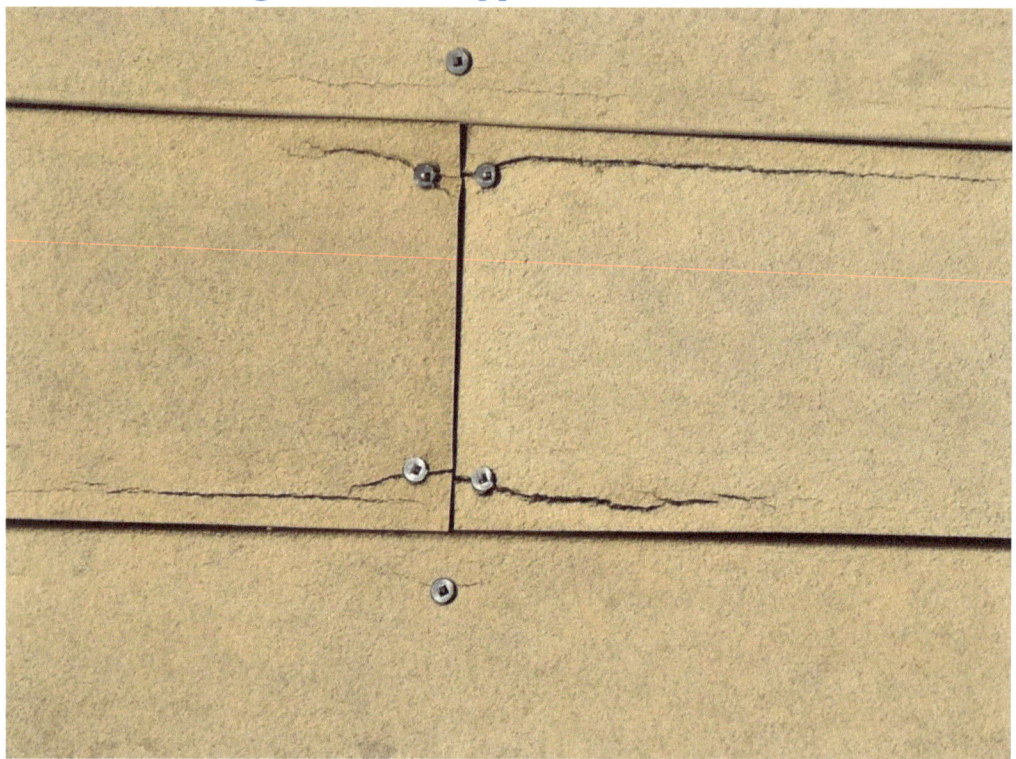

One of my readers sent me images of another plastic deck that is going to be replaced with timber. In this case the customer insisted on having plastic decking. We can assist you with evidence if you find yourself in this a predicament. The problems with timber are quite easily sorted and we can guide you through it. In case you missed it last month's newsletter showed a deck where timber was chosen over plastic.

F14 Appearance Grade or F17, Which is the Best?

One of our suppliers charges us the same price for F14 Appearance grade as he does for F17. Recently I was asked which one was better. For equal money, F14 appearance grade is most likely better purchasing if you are prepared to run the gauntlet of possibly larger knot size and it would be probably be stronger than an F17. But it is still not a perfect specification for many applications as it does not deal with heart and allows too large a knot for it to be used as handrail and decking. Most importantly it still does not deal with shrinkage, stability and durability. You will only get this by nominating one of the true royal species. See the November 2011 newsletter for how to specify handrails. below is a comparison of the two grades.

GRADE COMPARISONS APPLY TO SPOTTED GUM		
Fault	**F14 Appearance**	**F17**
Fractures and splits	Only end splits are allowed	Only end splits are allowed
Sawing tolerance	+ or – 3 mm	+ or – 3 mm
Unsound knots,	Not permitted	One quarter of face
Sound Knots	One third of the face	One quarter of face
Borer holes	unlimited (up to 3 mm)	20 per 100x100 mm (up to 3 mm)
Termite galleries	Not permitted	Enclosed - not permitted, open - as
Slope of grain	1 in 8,	1 in 10
Heart	Permitted in limited species to be	Permitted to be one ninth of cross
Tight gum veins	unlimited	Unlimited
Loose gum veins	Not permitted	One sixth of the length and 3 mm
Gum pockets	Not permitted	Length: Up to three times the width
End splits	One and half times width but not	Width but not exceeding 100 mm in
Checks	Up to 1 mm wide and one half the	Up to 3 mm wide and one third of
Rot	Not permitted	3 mm deep and 150x100 mm per 2.0
Want and wane,	Not permitted	One fifth of the cross section

Edgar Stubbersfield

December 2014 Newsletter

Why Does No-one Listen about 150x150
150x150, An Exception
CPD Points
More on Plastic Bollards

Why does no-one listen about 150x150?

Early this month I had a phone call from a sawmill that was in trouble over the supply of 150x150 posts. The client had ordered 150x150 F17 appearance grade and after reading somewhere on the web that 150x150 with heart in the centre was only fit for landscaping, he expected to receive heart free material. He then complained to the reseller when it arrived with heart in, the reseller complained to the mill who in turn came to me.

F17 just refers to the primary structural properties - i.e. is it strong enough to do the job and AS2082 allows heart in the common species cut in Queensland. F17 does does not say whether it is appropriate for the application. But this was supposed to be F17 **appearance grade**. But that does not help either. There is generally nothing subjective about this specification, you can put a tape measure on a natural feature in the timber and say - it passes or it fails, Heart centre is not one of the exclusions for appearance grade. So the person received what he ordered. Note that people are specifying ordering, cutting and selling this product without actually knowing what they are suppose to be supplied/supplying. Unfortunately the new definition of heart in AS2082-2007 is too subjective for me to understand.

AS2082 is clear when it says, in effect, that if you want heart free material you have to specify it that way. Now OSA knows **how to process this material to tame the heart** but people will not pay for it so what are your options

- Go to a laminated product which will not be made with a cyclic de-lamination resistant glue which I do not believe even exists on the market for this product,
- Use the 192x192 Pioneer Post from OSA.

As for 150x150 being only fit for landscaping, they were not reading what I wrote. I maintain it is not **even** fit for landscaping - at least quality public landscaping. The lead image is of a 150x150 where the designer had carefully specified heart free 150x150 (someone who did listen) but the contractor, presumably wanting to save $20 per metre, ignored the specification and purchased and installed heart in material.

150x150 An Exception

A few months back I was in Forest Hill (between Gatton and Laidley) visiting my favorite watering hole, no, not the Lockyer Hotel but Sorella's cafe (just down the street and well worth a dive in from the highway). Unfortunately a truck had driven into two of the corner posts of this heritage listed hotel and done considerable damage to the whole verandah. Queensland Heritage Restorations were finishing a high quality repair and I had a good talk to Shane Earle, a director of the company. He said that the timber had to be replaced like for like so the posts had to be in one piece. Now 100 years ago you could purchase a 150x150 heart free piece in a long length but not now. So in consultation with all parties the replacement pieces were cut from a recycled power poles with the heart in the centre. It was hoped by the parties concerned that the smaller aged timber might have produced a more stable heart. (it probably doesn't). Not ideal but the only thing that could be done. An informed compromise is not the same thing as ordering one thing and expecting another.

Timber Induction Course Eligible for CPD Points

The guidelines for Engineers Australia and the Board of Architects Queensland allow me to award CPD points for the induction course or individual presentations. These are available to deliver at your office or university.

Timber Preservation.
Hardwood Grading.
Timber Decks – Designing for Durability,
Utilising Small Diameter Hardwood.
The Seven Deadly Sins of Timber Design.

More on Plastic Bollards

In my September newsletter I had a discussion on plastic or hardwood bollards. I showed pictures of shiny new plastic bollards and 30 year old hardwood bollards opposite my house. I should have added this image of a bollard in the same park which was less than 10 years old. The star picket up the centre is there because soon after installation someone broke it off at ground line. The UV of course is getting to the plastic. And with a straight face people are telling me that plastic is better than hardwood!

If you are having trouble with your timber bollards you should be talking to me, It is very simple to get right and I can advise you. I have only ever had one batch of bollards that did not perform well, they were 150x150 with the heart in the centre supplied to a clients specification. I learnt a lesson that day.

2015

Edgar Stubbersfield

January 2015 Newsletter

Durability of Thermally Modified Wood
Feedback on 150x150
CPD Points
Dangerous Canberra Deck
Canberra Bollards

Durability of Thermally Modified Wood

Back in the late 80's I visited a friend in central Finland, an incredible place. My friend took me to see a the Petäjävesi Old Church which was nearby. This was not long before It was inscribed in the UNESCO World Heritage List. This church was built between 1763 and 1765 and the bell tower was built in 1821. We will come back to this in a short while.

After a CPD seminar last year I was asked to comment on thermally modified wood which is fairly common in Europe. I was also sent a brochure claiming the wonderful benefits of this product. What we can say about the product is that it does improve the stability of the softwoods it is used on but question whether you get better stability than you achieve with our dense hardwoods. The trade off for this increased stability is that the timber becomes brittle. You do get increased decay resistance but not enough to raise it to a H3 level. A claim of "higher durability" should not be confused with "high durability". But we also have to look to termite resistance and thermal modification offers no resistance to termites. Some studies have shown that termites actually prefer thermally modified wood! Here is a link to a report on modified timber.

The brochure cited some documents to prove the claim of higher durability but when I checked them they were all from Finland where you can have a 250 year old softwood church. Now that church has been repaired many times but I did see very old pine log cabins that were original. The point is that you cannot rely on European and particularly Finnish testing to base your decisions on. The climate is too different as are expectations. See the April 2014 newsletter where international durability ratings are compared. Durabilty 1 in Europe is rated as 5 years plus whereas for us it starts at 25 years.

Demand Australian testing before you commit to this product.

Feedback on 150x150 warning

Last month I included a warning, yet again about 150x150 hardwood. I received the following supporting feedback from Richard Forester of Richard Forester Timber Inspection. Please take the issue seriously.

"Heart in material should never be allowed unless 175mm or larger. Even that is probably not enough (Ted here: That is also our experience) but that is how the standard has been for many years. I was happy for the change (I.e. to allow heart in timber in all sizes for many species) provided the timber was seasoned.

The problem is if you test the timber green (destructive testing) the timber (That is the timber with heart in) will pass. If you test it dry it will pass. It appears nobody on standards took into account what can happen during seasoning. To suggest a piece of Blackbutt 100 x 50 can be sold as F17 with heart when green is ludicrous. You just end up with 2 50 x 50's. I and my inspectors refuse to pass any green timber to this new clause introduced in 2082 in 2007. . . . If AS 2082 is rewritten I will be pushing to have the new clause allowed for seasoned timber only."

Timber Induction Course eligible for CPD Points

The guidelines for Engineers Australia and the Board of Architects Queensland allow me to award CPD points for the induction course or individual presentations. The same goes for landscape architects. These are available to deliver at your office or university. Ring me for a quote on 0414 770261

Timber Preservation.
Hardwood Grading.
Timber Decks – Designing for Durability,
Utilising Small Diameter Hardwood.
The Seven Deadly Sins of Timber Design. .

Deck, Queen Elizabeth Drive Canberra

While on Christmas holidays I again visited the deck in our national capital near the High Court. Now you cannot fault the architectural intent, when you look at the aerial view, it is stunning.

But like our politicians down there keep reminding us, the devil is in the detail. And here we do have a very serious gremlin. The deck, in my opinion should not have been built as detailed. Let's have a look at the details. It is a timely to remember that whatever you put on paper people will fall over themselves to supply and build (and pass the buck back to you).

When I was asked to quote against the plans for this deck in early February 2005 I realised it did not stand a chance of being safe if there were not changes made. It was basic primary school maths. I then wrote to one the parties offering our assistance to make this deck a success. Of course no one wanted to know. Why would you listen to an old sawmiller when everyone else everyone else was happy to send truckloads of timber to site without question. So the deck got built without modification. On my next trip to Canberra in 2010 I went to inspect the deck and of course it did all that I said it would, it simply had to do. It should have been closed to the public long before my visit as the gaps were dangerous. I could find gaps of up to 18 mm easily. This is exactly the situation our Deckwood system was developed for and would not have happened if it had been followed.

By chance one of my readers told me in mid 2010 how he had an accident on that same deck when the bike he was riding dropped down between an even larger gap. Over the handlebars he went and was injured. I went to Canberra over Christmas and went to photograph the deck again to show how they had ripped up the deck and relaid it to make it safe. I was going to write a reminder on designing your gaps properly. I was appalled to see that those responsible had not done so, only placing solid barriers in front of the deck, each with a sign "dismount area". Not good enough! If it is unsafe for a cyclists, it is definitely also unsafe for a wheelchair, it is definitely unsafe for someone with a walking stick and the potential consequences for women with high heels doesn't bear thinking about. I can't see any solution other than to re-deck the area and then some bureaucrat will say it is all timbers fault and use some other even worse solution like plastic.

I offer a service where I check plans for obvious issues like those encountered here but too few people take it up to make it worthwhile persisting with. I would have done it for free back then! My book *Deck and Boardwalk Design Essentials* has a check list in the back to work through so to avoid these problems but except for notable exceptions I can't get designers unfamiliar with the timber to even purchase even that. I should have said something in 2010 but my cynicism made me think that bureaucrats will normally only respond to lawyers. Nothing has changed to cause me to think otherwise.

As for the seats, not a good look. They need not have looked like that if they were processed differently. Refer to my *Seven Deadly Sins of Timber Design* to see how to do this.

Canberra Bollards

When you step out of the airport at Canberra you can see an extremely attractive crash resistant bollards designed by Guida Moseley Brown Architects. They are everything a bollards should be, functional, incorporating timber and attractive. I would love to have something like this in our range. This is design at its finest.

Throughout the city I have never seen so many bollards but while they are functional and made of timber I would not say they are attractive. They are as cheap as is possible with little concession to the need to accommodate timber's weaknesses. Most did not have even a weathering cut on the top. My contacts in Canberra tell me that price rules there. You would have to look hard to find this type of very basic traffic barrier in Queensland

Edgar Stubbersfield

February 2015 Newsletter

3D Printing in 60 Seconds
A Reminder About 50 mm Joists
CPD Points
A Special Note for my Baptist Readers (and Historians)

3D Printing Explained in 60 Seconds

As many readers know I am excited about the potential for 3D printing. Dr Jennifer Loy has sent me a link to her 60 second introduction to 3D printing to share with you. **The address is** https://www.youtube.com/watch?v=goRDnAdhXSs It is going to be an everyday part of your profession at least for my younger readers. Refer to the February 2013 newsletter for information on 3D printed bollard tops. Refer also to the August 2014 for information on how to get started with 3D pribting.   Her contact details are in the back issues.

50 mm Joists - A Reminder

Split 50 mm joist   Screw working out

Following a recent consultancy involving a structure with 14# screws and 50 mm joists it is prudent to raise the subject of narrow joists again. My guides are very clear - If you are face fixing Deckwood it goes on a 75 mm joist, the screws are in a staggered alignment and fully predrilled. No ifs buts or maybes. Still I see people trying to re-invent the wheel and substitute 50 mm with a case just last month. If 50 mm was suitable we would have said so. It not that the narrower joist is not strong enough it is just that they do not work. The screws are in a straight line and so split the joist.

In the left hand images above taken at a boardwalk that is about 11 years old you can see how badly split the joist is. You will never fit another deck on it as internal decay will have started. The right hand image shows a screw in the same deck that is coming out (not clear - granted but trust me). The boardwalk has to be regularly inspected for these raised screws which are replaced with longer screws to avoid trip hazards. The cost of a trip and fall insurance claim causes the expense of an upgrade to a 75 mm joist to pale into insignificance.   But why lay out your joists at 450 mm like a domestic deck when the decking will normally span at least 600 mm? Use less joists with a wider spacing and the impact at construction is not significant. Alternately, use 50 mm and fasten from underneath (which is probably better).

Timber Induction Course eligible for CPD Points

The guidelines for Engineers Australia and the Board of Architects Queensland allow me to award CPD points for the induction course or individual presentations. The same goes for landscape architects. These are available to deliver at your office or university. Ring me for a quote on 0414 770261

Timber Preservation.
Hardwood Grading.
Timber Decks – Designing for Durability,
Utilising Small Diameter Hardwood.
The Seven Deadly Sins of Timber Design.
and a new one *Joints*.

A Special Note for my Baptist Readers (and Historians)

I have recently edited some documents for some friends and put them in book format. These documents cover the journey in the 1870's from Hamburg to Brisbane and then from Brisbane to the "howling wilderness" of Kalbar in Queensland by the Rev, Herman Windolf. The journals are fascinating reading and the emigration Museum in Hamburg couldn't believe their good fortune when they received a copy. Herman was the first German Baptist pastor to come to Queensland. The struggles and heartbreaks of our pioneers and their fortitude is beyond my comprehension. The Queensland State Library was a brilliant source of images - all free. The book can be purchased from Amazon, Barnes and Noble, and Book Depositary.

March 2015 Newsletter

Standards You Can Drive a Bus Through
A Real Life Ghost Story
CPD Points

Standards You Can Drive a Bus Through

I remember 1974 well, love was in the air and I did my courting on the upper-deck of the 414 bus going from Dorking to Capel in the UK. It is yesterday I can't remember well. On the subject of buses that brings me to of some of the standards that relate to timber. Sadly aspects of them will allow you to drive the 414 bus through them. Let us consider one of these bus routes.

AS 2082-2007 has a limitation to the amount of lyctus susceptible sapwood that can be supplied in any given piece timber which for most grades is 20% of the cross sectional area. This was overridden by Queensland and New South Wales in their respective timber utilisation acts which would not allow any susceptible sapwood to be supplied. These were acts with real teeth and because of that we did not breach them. Then in their wisdom both governments repealed their acts and the protection that went with them. The image on the right probably now meets the requirements of F14 in Queensland and New South Wales. Are you happy to specify such material?

Not all sapwood is lyctus susceptible and doesn't get turned to powder from the larvae but that does not change the fact that it is not durable if used externally. The image above shows decay in blackbutt sapwood. When the piece was freshly cut the sapwood is clearly visible but as it dries it is hard to tell sapwood from heartwood. Used internally as an exposed beam it will not give you any problems. Move it outside and had it been fitted int a joist hanger the potential for trouble is enormous. Now AS 2082-2007 has <u>no limitation</u> on the amount of sapwood if the timber is not lyctus susceptible.

So, when I went to companies and offered them proprietary products that took the mystery out of specifying timber and I was met with the response "We only specify Australian Standard products" I smiled and thought of the 414 bus. How foolish of me to provide solutions to problems they weren't aware of. There is a lesson here, ensure all your external timber is treated to H3. Another lesson is the value of a consultancy by myself even if it is just to cast an eye over timber detailing.

Many thanks to the individuals who supplied the images. Want to know more? purchase my book on timber grading.

A Real Life Ghost Story

When I wasn't on the 414, I spent a few years in England training for an entirely different profession. One night I slept in a magnificent Louis 16th four poster that came complete with its own resident poltergeist. I barely slept a wink that night. Not because of any banging of doors and rattling of chains but because of the uncomfortable round bolster pillow. I could understand a member of the French nobility with a seriously sore neck coming back and haunting that bed! (Forgive my poor attempt at humour, the situation was actually very serious).

That brings us to the subject of ghosting. A friend's friend had problems with white marks coming through the varnish on some stairs. "Ghosting," the owners were told by the painters, "not our responsibility" and you will have to pay a vast sum for it to be sanded back and re-coated. A closer look and you can clearly see a workman's boot mark. This appears to be damage to the film due to exposure to contaminants during drying of the coating. This can occur in two ways. If someone walked on the freshly sanded timber with contaminated shoes before coating or sometime after coating when the film may have been dry to touch be not cured. From that one image it is difficult to say which except that the marks are on the stringer too. So we either have a case of the headless workman busy in the witching hour or more likely the careless workman whose mind was not connected to his feet. Much the same thing when you think about it.

To help avoid this happening the Wood Flooring Association suggest

1. Seal the newly laid timber floor with the intended first coat (sealer or finish) prior to exposure to other trades etc. This will protect the timber from most substances, and as the coating used is the same as or compatible with the first coat being used there will not be any coating system issues. It is however important to address any acclimatisation issues prior to the application of the first coat.
2. Where an instance is likely or has previously occurred, suggest that the windows or glass providing the UV exposure are polarized or UV filter film is applied before finishing/refinishing, or as soon as possible afterward.

Here are some helpful links
http://www.atfa.com.au/downloads/42_Ghosting.pdf and
http://www.woodflooringassociation.com.au/login/downloads/%281%29Data_Sheet_Ghosting_March08.pdf

Timber Induction Course Eligible for CPD Points

Those offices that have been using my CPD services have found them useful and keep asking me to come back. These are serious talks with serious learning outcomes with a test at the end. Ring me for a quote on 0414 770261. The image was taken a few years back when I was lecturing to Architects in Addids Ababa University. I thoroughly enjoy doing it. Subjects available are:

Timber Preservation.
Hardwood Grading.
Timber Decks – Designing for Durability,
Utilising Small Diameter Hardwood.
The Seven Deadly Sins of Timber Design. And the latest, Joints

Edgar Stubbersfield

April 2015 Newsletter

Talking timber with Ted
Nail or Screw Domestic Decking?
Welcome to NSW LALC readers
Log Footbridge

Talking Timber with Ted

Timber construction and durability in external application has always been my passion and In particular to see timber used In a fit for purpose application and last a lifetime In all its glory. I have written several books on external timber design and application over the years and presented as guest speaker at many Seminars including Timber Queensland's on the topic. The full range of subjects I have available are:

Timber Preservation.
Hardwood Grading.
Timber Decks – Designing for Durability,
Utilising Small Diameter Hardwood.
The Seven Deadly Sins of Timber Design.
Joints and a new one under preparation
Architectural Battens

Nail or Screw Your Domestic Deck?

When I built my home in 1992 I used over 1000 metres of ironbark pencil round decking. Nobody thought of screwing decking then so I followed the Timber Queensland directions and used 50x2.8 galvanised bullet head nails. Now this deck is under a roof and I have to admit, they have worked acceptably. There are only two places where I have replaced the nails with screws. Where the nails are not working well is on the two outer boards where many have worked out (illustrated) and the landings, which are not covered. These have had to be re-secured with screws. Had this been an exposed deck it would have been a disaster.

Still we are seeing builders who are gun nailing their weather exposed decks and refusing categorically to screw them. The matter was settled a long time ago when the Forests and Wood Products Research and Development Corporation did withdrawal testing on a range of fasteners on different joists. The image below summarises the results. It is frightening how badly some of the gun nails perform. Two galvanised bullet head nail have an average withdrawal of 2.6 kN but the gun nails can be down to 1.2 kN. Notice how the bullet head held better than frequently recommended 50x2.8 galvanised twisted dome heads (1.9 kN). Two eight gauge screws gave 10.8 kN withdrawal.

	Hand Nail						Machine Nail											Screw
Shank	Plain	Screw	Ring	Plain	Plain	Plain	Plain	Screw	Screw	Screw	Screw	Screw	Ring	Ring	Ring	Screw	Screw	Counter
Head type	Bullet	Dome	Flat	Bullet	Bullet	Bullet	Flat	Dome	Dome	Dome	Dome	Dome	Dome	Dome	Dome	Dome	Dome	sunk
Nail material	HD-Gal	HD-Gal	HD-Gal	SS	HD-Gal	SS	HD-Gal	HD-Gal Ad	HD-Gal Ad	SS	SS	SS-Ad	HD-Gal Ad	SS-Ad	SS	HD-Gal	SS	SS
Size	50 x 2.8	50 x 2.8	50 x 2.8	50 x 2.8	65 x 2.8	65 x 2.8	50 x 2.5	50 x 2.5	50 x 2.5	50 x 2.5	50 x 2.5	50 x 2.5	50 x 2.5	52 x 2.5	50 x 2.5	65 x 2.5	65 x 2.5	8g x 50
Timber Joist	Hw	Sw	Sw	Hw	Sw	Sw	Hw	Hw	Sw	Hw	Sw	Hw	Sw	Sw	Sw	Sw	Sw	Hw
Test	1	2	3	21	4	22	5	7	20	8	11	9	10	13	14	15	16	19
Shank dia (mm)	2.8	2.9	3.0	2.8	2.9	2.8	2.5	2.5	2.5	2.5	2.5	2.4	2.5	2.5	2.5	2.5	2.5	-
Thread dia (mm)	-	3.1	3.1	-	-	-	-	2.7	2.7	2.7	2.7	2.6	2.6	2.6	2.7	2.8	2.6	4.1
Length to head (mm)	48	48	49	48	63	63	43	50	50	49	49	51	50	50	48	63	64	47
Ave. withdrawal (kN)	2.6	1.9	1.6	1.8	1.1	1.0	2.0	3.0	1.2	3.3	1.6	2.0	1.6	1.8	1.7	1.6	0.9	10.8

Now one of these gun nails performed better than the bullet head nail rating 3.3 kn. I had to do a job where we nailed over our head so I found out the brand of nail and purchased a few boxes. I had some left over so three years ago I gave them to someone to fix a deck under cover. How did they perform? Lets just say, the owner did not thank me. The boards creak underfoot, unlike the 23 year old deck fastened with bullet heads on my house.

What about concealed fixings? That is another newsletter sometime.

Welcome to New Readers from NSW LALC

This is the first newsletter that the NSW Local Aboriginal Land Council Readers will have received. We hope you find it relevant and stay reading for years. Below are links to two sacred site projects on our website where we have supplied infrastructure.

Nudgee Waterholes - Brisbane
Murong Gailinga Aboriginal RockArt Boardwalk

Log Footbridge

The cost of timber girders has risen so much, and their availability is getting so poor that it is almost better to go straight to steel. This is unfortunate as a well built log bridge is very durable bridges with minimal issues, especially when you do the abutments correctly.

I am getting very pessimistic about the footbridge market. I fear there will only be a change when a bridge collapses with someone on it. If you are considering a nailplated bridge we need to have a serious talk. When you see a bridge where the bottom has dropped straight out into the creek below you would have the same concerns as me. But then, that is out of someone else's budget.

Timber Newsletters 2014-2017

May 2015 Newsletter

Where is Timber Construction Headed
Wisdom of High Design Loads
I Need Help with Architectural Battens

Where is Timber Construction Headed

Image courtesy of Dennis Clark Photography   0408 459 242

A few weeks ago, a chapter I wrote on timber construction was sent off to the editors of the French publication, *Le Memento du Forestier*. This chapter was initially intended to be in three parts. The first dealt with construction using timber with minimal processing such as natural rounds. And what do you think of this heritage listed bridge built from natural rounds in 1885 at Coominya, not far from home? The piles are very impressive. How things have changed from then to now. Last month I complained that I had trouble purchasing 2 girders at 8 m for a footbridge.

The second part of the chapter looked at construction using semi processed (i.e. sawn) timber. The final part was to cover construction using modern highly processed timber and this was to be covered by my friends in the Department of Agriculture, Fisheries and Forestry. The editors in France decided to drop the third section! The reasoning was that timber technology is changing so radically that whatever is written will be relatively quickly out of date. I think they are right.

Those who think timber is yesterday's material should look closely and the radical advances that are being made. Many have not progressed in their thinking about timber beyond the "old rattler" country road bridges.

Wisdom of High Design Loads

This Anzac Day I was reminded of the wisdom of the high design loads for footbridges and other structures. In Gatton we have the normal march down the main street and then we all head off to the Weeping Mothers Memorial (not the traditional light horseman) for the ceremony. This involves crossing the railway line over the heritage design footbridge. It would not be possible to load the bridge any more than it is for a short time every Anzac Day, then it goes back to having virtually no one on it for the rest of the year.

The problem with most footbridges is that purchasers, who often are not qualified to assess the suitability of the product offered, look at price only and the fact that the bridge seldom will have anyone on them. But then one day someone organises a fun run across it and for a short time it is fully loaded. You cannot tell in advance which bridge needs the high loads and which one does not so you make them all capable of withstanding the unusual event.

Still we see footbridges being offered with a 3 kPA loading and the load factor not being published. If this happens to you show the salesman the door immediately. We are so used to structures being safe that we forget that they can and do fail like the one above where the deck dropped into the creek.

I need Help With Architectural Battens

I have been asked to develop a CPD session on architectural battens. Simple enough I thought until I looked into it. I need help from my readers. I need images, accounts of where they have worked and very importantly, where they have not worked and why. I need to learn what insights you have. Image courtesy of Architectus.

June 2015 Newsletter

Come and Inspect Timber Research Facilities
Feedback on Deficient Timber Standards
Why do I Bother?
Paint Systems for External Steel
New Book Being Written

Your Opportunity to Inspect Forestry Research Centre

Lock the date Wednesday 5th August into your diary and come down to the Blomfield Street Salisbury research facility of the 1.30 pm to 3.30 pm? If your career is ahead of you, not finishing like mine, you need to be very aware of the radical changes that are occurring in both timber supply and the products that will be made from it. Right at the cutting edge is Henri Bailleres and his remarkable team of scientists and technicians. Henri would love to show you around the facilities and discuss the new directions for timber. You will see:

Material testing laboratory,
Plywood facility
Kilns
Practical constructions
Vacuum drying
And lots more

You will have the opportunity to study the above shelter. What makes the above shelter impressive is not the design, though you have to admit Michael Dixon of UQ's architecture department has done a great job, (note no visible fixings) but it is the fact that it is built from 12 year old plantation hardwood! This shelter incorporates both laminated beams and LVL in hardwood.

If that is not enough reason we will finish up with a CPD session on the Seven Deadly Sins of External Timber Design. Phone me on 0414 770 261 for the RSVP.

Feedback on Being Able to Drive a Bus Through Timber Standards

In the March newsletter I wrote about timber standards that you can drive a bus through. When doing a CPD session recently I was told of a job where exactly the same thing happened I warned about. Deckwood was specified and the builder substituted with a lower priced timber that contained large amounts of untreated sapwood. It lasted four years and now the asset owner has lost all confidence in timber. He will probably do something unwise and replace it with plastic.

You specify Deckwood or approved equivalent for a reason and people substitute for a reason, and they are not the same reason. The approval process for a substitute must be followed to protect yourself, the public and your client. It is not something left to the whim of a contractor who, in this case, did not have the faintest idea what he was doing. We can help you honestly assess the differences.

Why do I bother?

I get so frustrated and disillusioned at times. Yet again we were beaten on price for a boardwalk. I happened to be driving past and saw the alternative so I thought I would have a look. Hardwood posts set in concrete, (one of my seven deadly sins) and the joists attached with galvanised triple grips (and it is in a floodway!). The very poor image above shows a boardwalk where the joists were fastened by triple grips and was washed off the bearers in a flood. I write my books, I do my CPD sessions and at the end of the day it almost always comes down to price not specification and best practice. One of the things I do in my consultancy service is check plans. It would have been money well spent.

Paint System for External Structures (Not a paid advertisement)

Timber has its limitations; reluctantly even I have to admit it. Ironbark is wonderful but you cant weld it yet though Henri and his team are probably working on that. There simply are times when you have to incorporate steel to lesser or greater degree. I once quoted to supply a new steel framed footbridge but lost the tender for, I understand, $2-300. The bridge that was purchased (illustrated above) instead was showing rust after only 6 months. This is not the result you should be aiming for or what we offered. I want to share with you how we get a long life from our steel painted structures.

The truss that was developed for me is a fully welded one piece construction which gives us the U frame action required under the bridge code. The above truss is 27 m long and was moved in one piece. Because these bridges are too large to fit in the galvanising bath we have to use a painted finish to get our corrosion protection. We were originally pointed to PSX 700 by PPG and we could not have been happier. This paint's genesis was from the coating systems used for the rocket launch facilities of NASA. This finish gives us:

High gloss retention
Equal to or better than galvanised protection
Very high adhesion properties
Good environmental outcomes
Damage can be touched up simply with a paintbrush
Grafitti wipes off with solvent.

Our contact in PPG is David Slinger 0459 823 768

So between robust steel sizes, high quality PSX 700 finish and Deckwood decking you should not be specifying anything less than one of my trusses. Thinking of allowing a lower priced substitute? check out and ponder the third image in last month's newsletter.

New Book Being Written

I started to accumulate so much material on Architectural Battens that I thought I would try to put it into book form. I fully expect to sell as many as six copies. If you have stories of Architectural battens, either successes or failures I would love to hear them so we can all learn. Am image of leaching from battens would be helpful. I need a good image of a clear film finish breaking down, can you help?

July 2015 Newsletter

When to Use Stainless bolts and Brackets
New Book Being Written

Dear Reader

When to Use Stainless Bolts and Brackets

Galvanised bolt after 12 months in spotted gum in Gatton

In light of the deteriorating performance of imported galvanised bolts (and they are all imported) and the wide divergence of opinion from different sources of when to use stainless fasteners, I thought it would be useful to give you my observations.

Species	pH	Trouble
Blackbutt	3.6	yes
Mountain ash	4.7	no
Ironbark red NL	4.0	yes
Spotted gum	4.5	no
Rose gum	5.1	no
Jarrah	3.3	yes
Radiata	4.8	no

Source: Embedded Corrosion of Metal Fasteners in Timber Structures FWPA Manual 6

Firstly you have to consider the acidity of the timber. Our hardwoods are all acidic. Spotted gum with a pH of 4.5 is outside of the problem area of 4.3 or less. So if you are just saying F14 hardwood and not being careful abut what species you accept, you must anticipate and design to avoid corrosion on your bolts. The new timber treatments are also more acidic than CCA and are more likely to corrode fasteners. But what are the recommendations?

Timber Preservers Association recommendation:

For higher corrosion resistance <u>in marine, salt or chemical environments</u> hot dipped galvanized nails and screws should be used. Hot dipped galvanising involves the application of a relatively thick sacrificial zinc coating by hot dipping in a zinc bath. The process leaves a rough surface with enhanced withdrawal and corrosion resistance characteristics.

Koppers Micropro

High Hazard Zones. These are zones that are up to 10km from a surf coast or up to <u>1km from a non surf coast</u> or near swimming pools, brackish water etc. In these zones Type 304 or Type 316 stainless steel hardware is suitable. The link is http://www.kopperspc.com.au/pdf/MicroPro%20hardware.pdf

Lonza

Copper Azole and CCA Treated Wood [1]

	Indoors Always Dry (<15% MC)	Protected From Weather Dampness OK	Outdoor In Weather Regular Wetting	Coastal Applications	Wood Foundation & Other Critical Applications
AWPA Use Category	UC 1	UC 2	UC 3, UC 4A	UC 3, 4, 5	UC 4B
Fasteners	Mild Steel, EP [2] HDG HDG per ASTM A153 MG per ASTM A695 Class 55 Copper 304/316 SS	HDG per ASTM A153 MG per ASTM A695 Class 55 Copper 304/316 SS	HDG per ASTM A153 MG per ASTM A695 Class 55 Copper 304/316 SS	304/316 SS	304/316 SS
Connectors – Light gauge steel	HDG [3] HDG - ASTM A653 Class G185 Copper 304/316 SS	HDG - ASTM A653 Class G185 304/316 SS	HDG - ASTM A653 Class G185 304/316 SS	304/316 SS	NA

Unlike Koppers Micropro, Lonza do not differentiate between surf coasts and non surf coast. They define coastal as within 8 km from the coast. Source: "Corrosion and hardware recommendations for treated wood" Arch Technical Note.

Pryda

DISTANCE FROM COAST	CORROSION ENVIRONMENT FOR COASTAL AREAS (see note below)	
	OCEAN COAST (Subject to Breaking Surf)	SHELTERED BAYSIDE (Not subjected to Breaking Surf)
Up to 100m	SEVERE MARINE	SEVERE MARINE
100m to 1 km	SEVERE MARINE	MARINE
1 km to 10 km	MARINE	MODERATE
Greater than 10 km	MODERATE	MODERATE

Table 1 – Corrosion Environments

LOCATION	CORROSION PROTECTION REQUIREMENT FOR DIFFERENT ENVIRONMENT		
	SEVERE MARINE	MARINE	MODERATE
INTERNAL	Z275 or equivalent [1]	Z275 or equivalent	No Protection Required [4]
EXTERNAL [2]	Marine Grade 316 stainless steel or equivalent [2]	Marine Grade 316 stainless steel or equivalent [3]	Marine Grade 316 stainless steel or equivalent [3]

Pryda are even more restrictive in the use of stainless. Even if the use is more than 10 km from the coast, if the use is external e.g. a verandah, it must be stainless.

When I was researching this issue in my Timber Preservation Guide (have you purchased your copy yet, and why not if you haven't) I asked the recommendations of another timber treatment supplier. It was referred back to their lawyers in the US. That company refused to give a recommendation and referred me to the bolt manufacturers recommendations - which don't exist. So you could be excused for finding this a difficult area to answer definitively and the implications are very serious. So, what is the answer?

To the rescue comes our New Zealand brothers. They built a series of timber "structures" using a variety of preservatives and screw types and put them in two locations, one just metres from breaking ocean and the other was in what was considered a benign application. They left them there for years to determine what actually happened. There were enough of these units that they could dismantle them to check at corrosion at regular intervals. Their finding in part was:

- Corrosion rates derived from accelerated tests performed at high temperature and high humidity cannot be extrapolated to predict the service life of a specific component exposed to real service conditions
- Given that average corrosion rates of mild steel and zinc-coated items measured were commonly two to three times higher with ACQ or CuAz treated timbers over CCA if the timber gets wet, it is doubtful that hot dipped galvanised nails or mechanically plated screws will be able to meet the durability requirements of the NZBC and relevant New Zealand standards. The use of either AISI 304/316 grades of stainless steel, or durable equivalents such as silicone bronze, for structural components and connections in ACQ and CuAZ treated timbers (H3.2 and above) to meet the 50 year durability requirement would appear to be a sensible interim precaution.

Their real life findings are more in keeping with the recommendations of Lonza and Pryda. A surprising finding was that the shank of the fastener (as opposed to the head) often corroded more in the benign environment than close to breaking sea! The green bars in the graph below is the site close to the ocean. Contact me for a copy of this report.

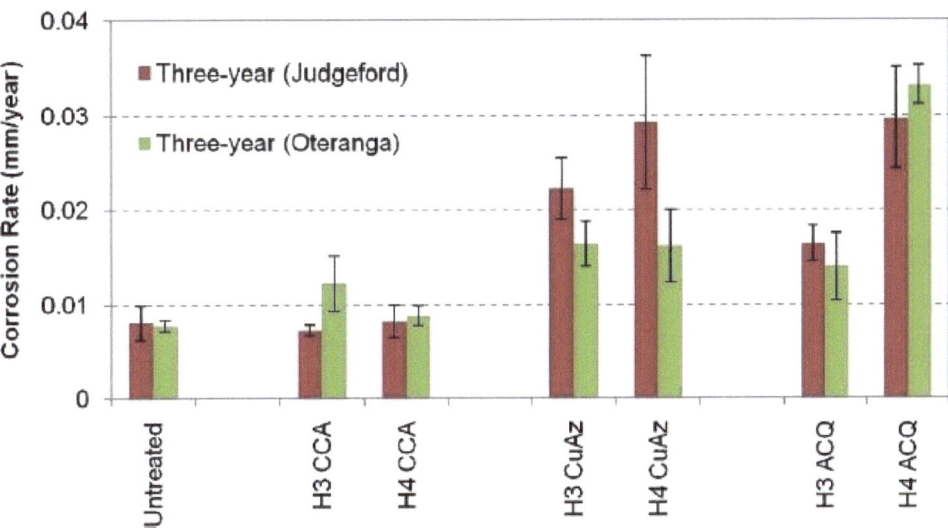

Figure 48: Corrosion rates of hot dip galvanised nails measured after three years of exposure at Judgeford and Oteranga Bay

The practical implications of this are enormous. A boardwalk and deck should be built with stainless fasteners but if you price on stainless you won't get any work!! I know that from bitter experience. That was long before last month I complained about being beaten on price on a boardwalk where the builder only used galvanised triple grips! But as most of my readers are specifiers you have the power to say, "I will only accept stainless". For new products such as our prestige bollards we are only using stainless fasteners.

New Book Almost Complete

My book on architectural timber battens is all but complete and is already at a useful stage if you need it. It will be $33. I still need a good image of a clear film finish breaking down, Can you help?

August 2015 Newsletter

New Publication Available
Images Sought for New Footbridge Book
How to ensure the Correct Varandah Joist Life
Forest Red Gum - Something I Just Noticed

New Publication Now Available

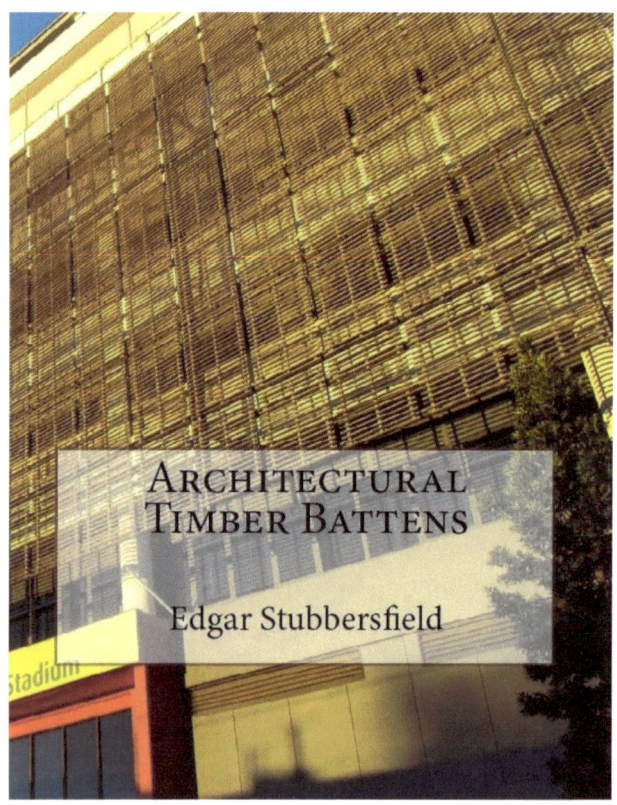

What is the difference between a project using battens that look great, age well with minimal maintenance and one that is a maintenance nightmare? The answer is $44, the cost of my latest book, *Architectural Timber Battens* which is now available for purchase. Better still It is available this month only for $33 but will be increasing to $44 next month. It is very good value as this book has tapped into the expertise of some of the countries leading timber consultants, scientists and architects. It includes everything you need to know and has a number of case histories. There should not be an architectural practice without this book.

Need a hard copy? You can purchase this from Amazon, Barnes and Noble, and Book Depositary. Why not lash out and purchase the books you need for your library before Tony puts GST on them (and dare I say, put some food on my table).

Images Sought for New Book

Timber Footbridge at Windsor UK

I am well under way on my sixteenth book since semi retiring (not all are on timber). That doesn't count the eight guides written previously. This latest guide deals with footbridges. Now, I already have a guide on footbridges and it tells you what to build. This new book primarily deals with How. I have about 50 pages put together including 20 on handrail. I am looking for images and hope my readers can help me. What I am particularly looking for are

- Bridge failures
- Non durable hardwood decaying
- Termite damage

If you have these images and others that you would like to share with me I would be grateful to receive them.

How to Ensure the Correct Verandah Joist Life

(Image used with permission)

If you are a Queenslander, you would have to have been living under a stone not to be aware of the fatal deck collapse at Hamilton. The 90 year old timber did not fail, it was a construction mistake from that long ago that eventually made its presence felt. Weather exposed timber design does not forgive any error. Today anyone designing a deck, and anyone building a deck and anyone certifying a verandah or exposed deck should immediately hear warning bells and proceed with the utmost caution. But it seems that the captain of the Titanic is at the helm and it is full steam ahead and the lessens have not been learnt. Why this note of despair? The rotten joist is on a large deck that is less than eight years old, If that was not enough, the bearer is Tasmanian oak and it is going the same way.

This is not rocket science. I was thrown out of school at grade 10 and even I can get my mind around it. You do not have to have an encyclopaedic memory nor do you do not have to have second sight to explore the esoteric mysteries of the universe, you just need to be able to read. (I had 52 in my class and still managed this skill). The nationwide Building Act 1975 gave legislative authority to the comprehensive provisions for the design and construction of homes and other structures called the Building Code of Australia (BCA). By referencing related companion documents such as Australian

Standards, they were no longer a voluntary code but also had the force of law. In Queensland one of these companion documents is the two volume Construction Timbers in Queensland. In the first volume it mandates a 50 year design life for verandah joists, not seven years. But how do you plan to get to 50 years, and you have to plan? That is where the second volume comes in. It lists all the species you are likely to encounter and tells you authoritatively if a given species is suitable or what has to be done to make it suitable. All of this is free of charge off the net. What's more, it is the end of the matter as it is the law. Follow its recommendations and you have planned to succeed. Let's look at a couple of specifications for joists where designers have not planned to succeed.

F14 Hardwood. As much as 85% of the production from Queensland state forests are from the most durable group of species that we call royal species. But that same group of highly durable timber only makes up 20% of NSW forestry production. But then you could put your faith in the lowest tenderer to have purchased the more expensive species. All you are saying with F14 is in effect that the piece will a permissible working stress in bending of 14 mPA. Almost useless information. It says nothing about durability stability shrinkage or appearance. You have to be precise in your species. I would not use blackbutt and F14 is a very low grade indeed in anything decent. Fortunately most, but not all, suppliers give you better

F17 KD Hardwood. This is a higher F rating so it has to better - right? Wrong!! When timber is dried it increases in strength. An F14 GOS spotted gum jumps two grades and becomes F22 when dry. Generally speaking F17 KD is a very low spec in anything with respectable durability properties. For spotted gum, again, it has about 40% of the strength of clear timber. For Ironbark it is off the scale anything that was conceived that anyone would ever sell. Again there is no durability as it is either a good species of appalling quality or it is a non durable timber such as Victorian ash of reasonable quality.

All this is explained in my books *Grading Hardwood - Understanding AS2082*. The possibility of getting this wrong is why we developed Joistwood - so you would not have to understand all of this. When we supply joists we give you what you need. If you are a building designer you need to invest the $33 that that book costs or purchase a hard copy from Timber Queensland. Still not convinced? Here is some additional reading:

F17 is an almost useless specification Jan 2013 Newsletter
Decks that can Kill February 2010 Newsletter

Forest Red Gum – Something I Just Noticed

I have in the past used forest red gum for boardwalk joists. A good piece went F17 and it was durability Class 1 in ground. It should d have been good. I was checking on something else recently and I saw that its strength has been re-classified. Earlier Structural Grade 2 went F14 and Structural Grade 1 went F17. Structural Grade 1 is the highest grade. Now both grades only meet F14. That rules FRG out for joists for boardwalks and decks.. It did not work as decking.

Edgar Stubbersfield

September 2015 Newsletter

New Publication Being Finalised
Fence Images Sought
Using Laminated beams externally
Using LVL beams externally

New Publication Being Finalised

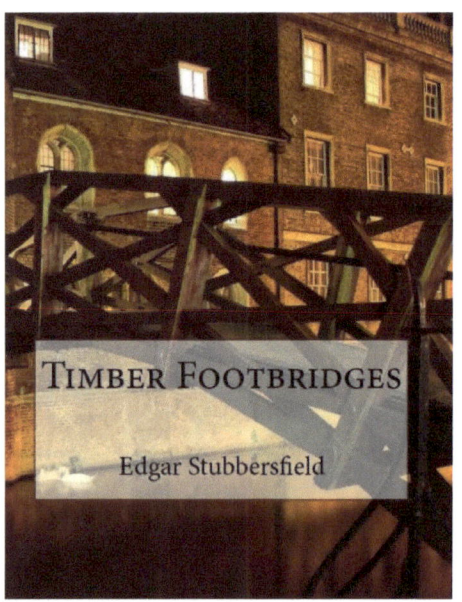

I have been working on the latest book in my Timber Design Files series, *Timber Footbridges*. Do you have any images that might help? There are over 140 images so far. Despite being a much bigger book than the last one, *Architectural Timber Battens*, this has been much easier. With the footbridge book I have had experience from 1984, and an embarrassment of riches when it came to images and other information. If you are designing a bridge now, the book can be used in its present form. Incidentally, the cover image is from the Mathematical Bridge in Cambridge. For more on this famous bridge see the April 2012 newsletter

This is one of the images from the book. A log girder Finke truss bridge near Yamba over Alligator Creek which spanned 36 m and was in service for 70 years. For those of you who love concrete and steel, consider, what material other than timber can give a ten fold increase in its design load and continue to give good service.

Fence Images Sought

The next book might be on fences. This fence fell over due to the posts being set in concrete and the decaying. So there probably is a call for this book as well. Do you have any images you would like to share with me. I am looking for images showing good practice, bad practice and remarkable fences. In the meanwhile, if you want to do a good job with your fence, talk to me.

Using Laminated Beams Externally

Image used with permission

When you use a Tasmanian oak laminated beam externally there can be only one possible outcome and it is not a good one. You can only scratch your head and wonder how a building designer, building certifier and an alleged specialist deck builder could see no problem using a durability 3 above ground timber in an exposed application, laminated beam or not. But it did have a strength rating and, far to often, people think that if it has a strength rating it must therefore be durable. They also confuse quality products with appropriate products. Because of this you end up with expensive rectification as this job will require. This beam would have been a premium product if used internally. But how do you use a laminated beam externally?

The first image shows the consequence of using non durable timbers externally, This image shows the danger of using glues that are not cyclic delamination resistant externally - there are straps holding iot together. How can you tell what glue you have? It is very easy, to my knowledge all the beams with the better glue are imported. However <u>Hyne give good guidance on how to make the standard beam work</u> if you have to use them. Obviously you must choose the most durable timbers but that is just the start. further requirements are:

1. The use of arrised or round edges on beams to reduce the likelihood of coating failures on sharp edges.
2. The use of drip edges or other devices which provide a path for free moisture flow away from the timber beam.
3. Shielding of the beam from free moisture or direct sun. The use of metal, fibro or plastic shields on the exposed faces or ends of beams is required to help maintain the beam in an unstressed dry condition. Refer to their TDS for a diagram.
4. Joists and Bearers in weather exposed (above ground) decks shall be installed and protected. Refer to their TDS for a diagram
5. The use of damp proof membranes is also required where the beam may be in contact with moisture through porous masonry or concrete.
6. All beams shall be provided with adequate ventilation so that moisture content within beams will not exceed 15% and moisture gradients across the beam will not occur.

JOINT DETAILING SHOULD, WHEREVER POSSIBLE, COMPLY WITH THE FOLLOWING:
• Keep horizontal contact areas to a minimum, in favour of self draining vertical surfaces.
• Ventilate joint surfaces by using spacers, wherever possible.
• Always use compatible fasteners which have adequate corrosion protection and do not cause splitting during installation eg. hot dipped galvanic coatings or stainless steel.
• Ensure any moisture entering a joint is not trapped but can adequately drain away from the joint. Refer to their TDS for a diagram
• Allow for thermal expansion/contraction in the joint design.
• The use of building overhangs and other structures which protect the beams from excessive moisture movement and sun exposure
It is probably easier to wait for the mill to cut a piece of solid timber in spotted gum or ironbark and design for the shrinkage.

Using LVL Joists Externally

Image courtesy of Alex Fleri of Original Decking

The H3 treated LVL verandah joist in the image above was only 18 months old when it was replaced with solid treated pine. The fasteners split the joist, moisture enters and it is all over. The less expensive beams are treated after laminating meaning the moisture is going directly into what can be untreated pine. The more expensive beams are laminated after treating which should take longer to decay but the outcome is likely to be the same.

The same technical data sheet from Hyne is very clear. It is an unsuitable use of their product if the " LVL if surface is exposed horizontally to the weather and water entrapment can occur." The same can be said about any brand. Unsuitable = don't do it. It gets back to the same issue of a quality product not always being an appropriate product. (Hyne information is used with permission).

Edgar Stubbersfield

October 2015 Newsletter

New Publication is Finalised
Bollards - Let the Buyer Beware
Fence Images Sought

New Publication is Finalised

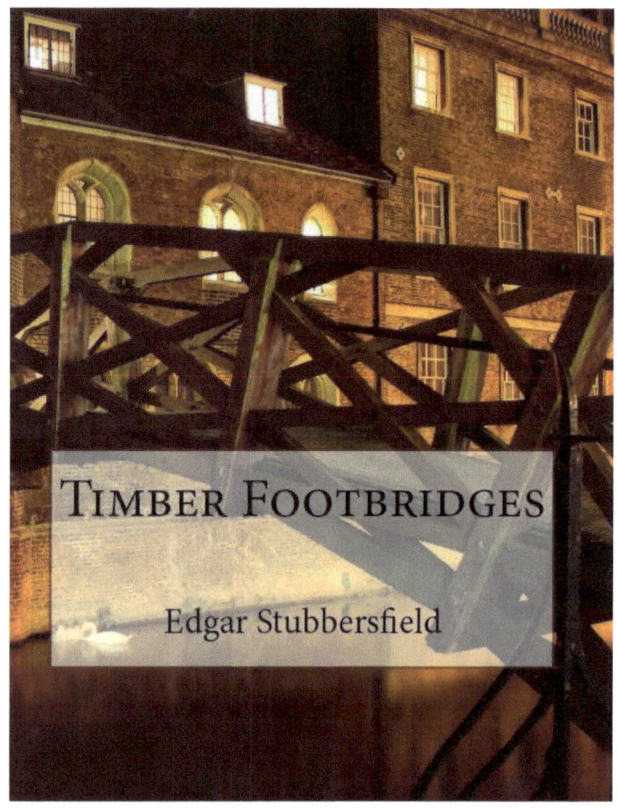

The latest book in my Timber Design Files series, with over 140 images, *Timber Footbridges,* is complete. The cover image is from the Mathematical Bridge in Cambridge. For more on this famous bridge see the April 2012 newsletter You can purchase the PDF from the author for $50 or purchase a hardcopy from Amazon, Barnes and Noble, and Book Depositary.

This is one of the images from the book. We think of cable stayed bridges as something new and post 1950 but this bridge was built over the Logan River in Queensland in 1880 and was in service for over 65 years. For those of you who love concrete and steel, consider, what material other than timber can give a ten fold increase in its design load and continue to give good service. Oh, and for my interstate readers, this bridge and the 36 m Finke truss from last month appear to only have been made in Queensland. Perhaps they were right about us living in the "smart state" even that far back.

Bollards - Let the buyer beware

One day I was walking in the park opposite my home when I happened to see a friend. I asked him how he was, "Not very good" was the reply. Then I saw what had happened. His dear wife had hit the accelerator not the brake and driven into one of my 30 year old Heavy Duty series traffic barrier posts. There was sufficient damage to write the car off. That is the performance you can expect from a good hardwood bollard or post. I have been watching these posts and rails over the years and the only thing that needed modification was a water shedding profile to the top of the rails and some other minor incremental changes (e.g. pencil rounding instead of chamfering) we have introduced over the years.

We produce a good product but not everybody is willing to pay what it costs to do it properly. Our main customers are councils and state government who are interested in purchasing product that ages gracefully with minimum maintenance, not contractors maximising the profit that can be made (there are exceptions of course). I was very disappointment recently when, in my travels, I came across a project where timber bollards were used. But the disappointment was not because a local supplier didn't get the order but because of the quality of the timber, the treatment and the apparent installation practice. Consider these nine images.

CCA treatment label   Water ring, end split and close to heart   Close to the heart

Included heart	End split and close to heart	End split and close to heart

Gum vein and close to heart	Close to heart	Gum vein and close to heart

If the appalling timber quality and the CCA treatment wasn't enough it was compounded but here was evidence that the posts were set in concrete!, That is something you never do with hardwood. Incidentally, these images are representative, not the total.

The type of material we are looking at is what you would expect if someone purchased landscaping timbers (no quality control and cut to the heart) grown in a higher rainfall area such as northern New South Wales. Who would blame the assert owner if they said, "If this is how timber behaves we will never use it again.." People who have not been trained in timber can be forgiven for not being aware but there is plenty of information available on how to do it correctly. Two of the seven deadly sins in my book and CPD session of that name cover what went wrong here. An investment of $22 could have stopped this!!! Who is primarily at fault is the sawmiller, but only if these were sold as bollards not landscaping. You cannot produce timber for years and not be aware of how the species in your region will perform and know the consequence of included heart. Once again the timber industry is its own worst enemy.

A few years back I got so sick of my bollards being specified and substituted with this type of material that I had a firm of very good landscape architects design a range of bollards that were hard to copy. This would protect our customers who had the faith in us to specify our product. The Eclipse range of bollards is one of these designs. Have you purchased my bollard guide yet? - Only $22.

Fence Images Sought

The next book will be on fences. Thank you Colin for this pic. Do you have any images you would like to share with me? I am looking for images showing good practice, bad practice and remarkable fences. In the meanwhile, if you want to do a good job with your fence, talk to me. A few years ago I rebuilt my side fence and the contractor complained about my requirements, which were things that he had never done before. I was only following Timber Queensland's technical data sheet on fencing.

Particular images I need are:

Old pine fence in the south that is faring well
Old cypress pine fence in the south. I am particularly seeking an image showing the sapwood decaying.

Edgar Stubbersfield

November 2015 Newsletter

Ted Has Found Something More Durable than Deckwood
Designing for the Local Climate
Expert Witness
Some Basics about Boardwalks/Decks
Writers Block - It Is Real

Ted Has Finally Found Something More Durable Than Deckwood

The Taj Mahal, Agra, India Completed 1653

The "Treasury", Petra, Jordan commenced 1st century AD

I recently had the opportunity to travel to India and Jordan to see friends and family members. There was no Indiana Jones, no rolling heads and no holy grail at the "Treasury" in Jordan, a bit of a disappointment really (apologies to those who have not seen the movie). The Taj took our breath away and left us wondering how such incredible beauty can exist side by side with what at times is unspeakable squalor and poverty. I begrudgingly had to admit that, yes, there are more durable materials to use than Deckwood and Joistwood.

For those of you who do not have access to 20,000 skilled but poorly paid artisans (getting one skilled craftsman is hard enough now) we have to set our sights a little lower. Deckwood will give you the maximum durability of any timber product when used in accordance with our design guides. You do not get this certainty when just cobbling together almost meaningless and often misunderstood terminology from various Australian Standards. Talk to me to find out more or better still, purchase the books.

Designing for the Local Climate

I have been criticised for having a Queensland focus in my books and newsletters. You can't accuse me of that this time. When in Jordan we went to see the alleged baptism site of Jesus on the Jordan River. While there, we parked under this shelter made of Oregon pine. It obviously has been there for some time yet the legs, which are set in concrete, are in good condition! It would be on the ground in a very short time in Queensland. What is the difference? It seldom rains but we did have a big dust storm.

Why the Queensland focus, for which I plead guilty? It is not just that we are the "Smart State" as our political masters tell us. Queensland's climate varies dramatically and includes hot wet tropics, interior deserts and a warm temperate to cold interior, all combined with high UV. You have to be smarter than a Jordanian Landscape Architect (at least) to develop systems that work in Queensland but once you have them they will then work anywhere. The performance in Victoria will be even better. But If you have something that works in Victoria, quite possibly it cannot be exported to Queensland. In my semi retirement (or is that retirement? I am writing this on my 65th birthday) I have tried to put in writing what I have learnt over a lifetime so it does not have to be learnt again. Still we see people ignoring the help that is out there and trying to reinvent the wheel and making the same basic mistakes. It is awfully frustrating.

Expert Witness

I am dipping my toe in the very muddy field of expert witness work. If you think I can be of assistance please contact me on 0414 770 261. I can write a very reasonable report

Some Basics about Boardwalks/Decks

It is almost impossible to sell appropriate product now. Price is almost always chosen before fitness for purpose. Consider the top left hand image. The boardwalk joists are held down with lightly galvanised multi grips. The manufacturer of this brand requires stainless when used externally. On the practical side you do not get a good enough connection to easily straighten a 75 mm wide joist. The manufacturer also advised that they have not tested this product for this type of application so it is being used outside of its guidelines. The picture directly under shows a boardwalk held down with triple grips that was washed off the bearers. The failed boardwalk was replaced with one of ours. (Anybody got a better image of a failed triple grip?).

The image on the top right shows the post which is hardwood and set in concrete. This is something you should never do as it promotes decay at groundline - see the image directly below. If you are going to use hardwood posts, use it in conjunction with no fines concrete, fine crushed rock or natural earth. The treatments seem to work far better on pine than hardwood. Although pine is a four letter word to me, its use in boardwalk foundations is probably the best thing you can do.

I spoke about reinventing the wheel. When my son had an aptitude test for his grade 11 courses, he was shown a similar figure to the bike above. The student before him nailed it right away. It had no hand brake!! Got it in one. That what happens when you try to reinvent something that is already sorted. You run the risk of designing something with square wheels. The two problems I show above are addressed in my Timber Preservation Guide - see treatment and corrosion and posts in concrete, and my deck and Boardwalk Design essentials guide where I discuss joist to bearer attachment. A grand outlay of $66. The grips, the posts and not investing in some research lowered the cost to build so I suppose that is all that matters.

Writers Block - It is real

The next book will be on fences - eventually. I have to admit, I am having writers block. Not like me at all. But what do you think of this fence (image courtesy of Keighron Fencing in the UK). The rail is a split 75x75 which gives good water shedding and good thickness in the centre for fasteners. Does anyone know of this type of rail being used commercially in Australia. I expect my hardwood would not stay straight. Do you have any insights to share.

Particular images I need are:
Old pine fence in the south that is faring well
Old cypress pine fence in the south. Particularly seeking an image showing the sapwood decaying.

December 2015 Newsletter

Same Plans - Two Different Products
Expert Witness
What Does a London Bus Have in Common with my Bridges?
Decay in Treated Pine
Writers Block - It Is Real

Same Plans - Two Different Products

Custom post made by the author.	Lower price substitute used in next stage.

Our consulting engineer once told me "There is a lot less information in the plans that I prepare for you compared to the ones I give others". He explained how over the years he understood our fabrication processes so it would have all been superfluous. When you do not have this control and confidence, which you can't have when landscaping goes to public tender, you have to detail your plans so there is no "wriggle room". If the designer has a high expectation he/she should provide more than basic dimensions but provide fabrication details as needed to achieve the finish envisaged. A well detailed commercial product does not happen by accident with the lowest price tenderer! The two figures above illustrate how two very different aesthetics and qualities can be achieved from the one set of plans.

To assist you in assessing the extra information needed consider the differences between these custom bollards are:

- Sleeve nuts versus countersunk nuts
- Timber processed then treated versus treated then processed
- Tanalith E/ACQ versus CCA
- Grooved, assembled and then the tops cut versus all theoretical measurements
- One set in no fines concrete (not visible from image) and the other not, and
- Dimensions sanded off versus dimensions left on timber

Expert Witness

I am dipping my toe in the very muddy field of expert witness work. If you think I can be of assistance please contact me on 0414 770 261. I can write a very reasonable report

What does a London Bus have in Common with my Bridges?

I don't know how they did it but it seemed to always happen. I would queue at a bus stop in London for what seemed an eternity for a Number 19 bus (not for Soho but the British Museum) and then, all of a sudden, four would turn up in convoy. It is almost as if the old Routemaster had an inbuilt herd instinct.

We had a London bus experience this month when we shipped out three of the Warren truss bridges that were developed for me (see below). These three bridges were all sold to developers and were specified by wise engineers. We should really be doing it every month but everything is working against it with what I see as often very poor tender procedures from many local governments. When I see a council tender request now I can almost certainly say it is pointless quoting. At most what you usually receive is a satellite image with a rectangle drawn on it showing the length and position of the bridge. There usually is no cross section of the crossing, definitely no soil test, invariably no hydraulic information. Every tenderer is expected to obtain this before submitting the price. Every bit of responsibility is moved to the supplier and the cost blown out in the process through making assumptions in the supplier's favour. When there is an issue, trying to find 30 year old documentation, from companies that are probably no longer in business, is next to impossible so the responsibility comes back fully on the council in the end.

The most important thing about bridges is to purchase well and that starts with a very tight specification. In my book, Timber Footbridges, I have a chapter on the tender process including a specification and checklist. If you can't afford $50 for the book I will send you that chapter for free. If you have seen what I have over the years you would understand my concerns.

The bridge where the sign to your left was installed and can be seen at this link had the best prepared tender documentation I had ever seen. The plans were not checked prior to receiving the bridge. You have to follow through which is why I developed the checklist.

This article is already too long. If you want to know why you should be specifying one of my truss bridges see this link to the June 2014 newsletter or call me on 0414 770 261. Take special note of the paint we use. It is absolutely brilliant. The decking in the bridge below is of course

25m truss at retirement village - Gold Coast - Installed Dec 2015

18 m truss bikeway installed at Landsborough in Dec 2015

20 m truss installed at Cooroy Dec 2015 - an OSA boardwalk will attach to both ends

Decay in Treated Pine

Recently at a CPD session I was asked about the durability of treated pine. The questioner told a story of a large job where treated pine was specified and used in accordance with the manufacturer's recommendations. The timber decayed and the rectification cost was staggering.

Treating pine is no guarantee of success, just as it isn't with hardwood. Consider the two packs of sleepers above. You can easily see that only a small part of the timber is actually treated. the heart of pine is just as untreatable as the heart of hardwood. The outside of the two packs is coloured green but not the bulk of the inside. It is still durability class 4 material being used where you need a class 1 and simply has to fail. The maximum amount of untreated heartwood should not exceed 20% but in these cases above it is probably 80%. This is why treated pine can decay.

If I was purchasing significant amounts of pine I would require the timber to be incised to a depth of 10 mm and treated to H4. The incising process allows the chemicals to penetrate the heartwood and the extra chemical cost is not significant.

Writers Block - it is real

I am still making hard weather of the fencing book. The book includes specifications so you avoid problems like the one above. Do you have any insights to share with me?

Timber Newsletters 2014-2017

2016

Edgar Stubbersfield

January 2016 Newsletter

Large Price Reduction for Deckwood
Timber Fence Book Finalised
Why so Hard to do the Right Thing? - Very important article
Decay in Treated Pine

Large Price Reduction on Deckwood

My lovely wife, Rachel, who holds the IP on Deckwood, has decided that we will take the marketing of Deckwood back in house. That IP does not expire till 2019. The new manufacturers have given me revised pricing to our specification and profile and that will see a very big reduction in price despite a small royalty being paid to her. There is a new website being prepared www.deckwood.com.au which will be up and running in a couple of weeks. Please bookmark that address for future reference.

We have decided to make the Boardwalk Design Guide and the Deckwood selection Guide free again on the website, long overdue. My role will be as it has been for many years now, to advise you on how to use it correctly. There will be more information about my consultancy services on the new website but basically if you specify Deckwood I do not charge. The trade name Deckwood and the Registered Trade Name LifePlus is also held by my wife.

Guess which project got input from me?

It really does make a difference when you get us involved. We know our craft well and we can help you to avoid the things that cause premature degrade of a weather exposed timber structure. You can tell the difference between a structure with my input and one that does not. We would be the only people who would tell you that that our product should not be used when it is inappropriate.

Timber Fence Book Finalised

For some reason, this latest book has been all blood sweat and tears but finally it is near enough to being completed to sell copies. The cost is only $33 but you really should purchase the full set of all my guides. The book covers hardwood, cypress and pine fences.

You can't be vague in an area where there are no standards, widespread ignorance among contractors and a huge variation of quality and performance. If you are a professional designer who has to provide certainty and repeatability in your fence designs, you need this book!

Do you like the fence on the front cover? It is a pity you have to go to Japan to find designers who appreciate the possibilities of spotted gum combined with customers who will pay for it. Image courtesy of Kurata Co. more of their fence work can be seen at http://www.ecowood.or.jp/item/fence/index.html I would like to hear of good fence projects that can be added as case histories. What is next? Joints?

The following article, of critical importance to all specifiers, was written by Jack Norton, National Secretary of the Timber Preservers Association of Australia (TPAA). It was originally published in TPAA's January Contact magazine and is reprinted with permission.

Why so Hard to do the Right Thing???

As the name implies, vacuum pressure impregnation of timber involves putting wood into a pressure vessel and applying some combination of vacuum and pressure in order to achieve complete sapwood penetration. Apart from envelope treatment for termite protection, all specifications in Australian Standard AS1604.1 (the solid wood Standard) require all the sapwood to be penetrated. Sapwood and heartwood are described in TPAA's Technical Note 3 but an easy way to think about how a tree is built is to think of wood as a clump of drinking straws. The straws around the outside are unblocked and allow dissolved food and water to travel up and down the stem. This is the sapwood and in a freshly felled tree is full of liquid sap. The straws on the inside or the heartwood zone are blocked with resins and waxes that stop the passage of liquid.

Logs are most often cut up when they are green or full of sap and the resulting sawn product is called 'green-off-saw'. Because the sapwood is full of sap, green-off-saw material is extremely hard, some would say 'impossible' to treat properly to meet the specifications in AS1604.1. It is impossible to get preservative solution into the cells or fluid pathways that are already full of liquid. It is like trying to pour a beer into a glass that is already full of water. The best practice to treat green-off-saw material is to dry it before preservative treatment. This is more important with sawn pine compared to sawn hardwood. However, by far the majority of treatment plants treating products such as fence palings, fence rails or landscape sleepers treat the material without any pre-drying.

Why...???... because "if I don't treat it the bloke down the road will" and we wonder why we are losing market share to plastic and the alternate building materials! Why does one supplier condition timber before treatment and another does not? Often, sawmillers shipping green-off-saw timber know that the material they are supplying to timber treaters will undergo a treatment process, but justify their action by saying: "we haven't done anything wrong because we have marked it as green-off-saw." Whilst this may be true (and legal) is it the right thing to do?? I wonder who will get to the bottom first???

Decay in Treated Pine

Recently at a CPD session I was asked about the durability of treated pine. The questioner told a story of a large job where treated pine was specified and used in accordance with the manufacturer's recommendations. The timber decayed and the rectification cost was staggering.

Treating pine is no guarantee of success, just as it isn't with hardwood. Consider the two packs of sleepers above. You can easily see that only a small part of the timber is actually treated. The heart of pine is just as untreatable as the heart of hardwood. The outside of the two packs is coloured green but not the bulk of the inside. It is still durability class 4 material being used where you need a class 1 and it simply has to fail. The maximum amount of untreated heartwood in pine should not exceed 20% but in these cases above it is probably 80%. This is why treated pine can decay.

If I was purchasing significant amounts of pine I would require the timber to be preconditioned, incised to a depth of 10 mm and treated preferably to H4. The incising process allows the chemicals to penetrate the heartwood and the extra chemical cost for H4 is not significant when weighed against the cost of failure. Many Australian purchasers do not know what incising is and the image on the left shows what incised timber. In some overseas markets it is very common, western USA users expect external timber to be incised and it is becoming increasingly common in the UK. The pattern on the post illustrated is not the modern high intensity system which is preferred – (Check the Excalibur system from the UK)- which is arguably the best on the market. The incisions on this post was only 6 mm deep and I only got 6 mm penetration when I needed 10 mm. Always specify and check the depth of incision. For more information on incised pine or incising machines talk to Greg Jensen of Arch Timber Protection on 0419 329 006 or email greg.jensen@lonza.com

Edgar Stubbersfield

February 2016 Newsletter

A Reminder about Hardwood Posts in Concrete
Report on Timber Queensland Seminar, February 25
Fencing Brackets
Fence Book Completed
What Do You Do with a Good idea
How to Get More People to Specify Your Products
A Mortgage Broker that Helped Me

A Reminder About Hardwood Posts in Concrete

A reader recently sent me this image commenting that whoever put this post in does not read my newsletters. Hardwood and concrete do not mix. I have seen ironbark rot of at groundline in 14 years when set in concrete. Remember, use natural earth if suitable, fine crushed rock or no fines concrete. This is one of my "Seven Deadly Sins". So, seeing how easy it is to go wrong with a timber post, wouldn't it be better to use steel?

Well, No! It is even easier to do things wrong with steel. This image, supplied by David Tacon of Allinspect, shows a rusted steel post. He told me that this will be the second time the steel posts will have to have been replaced in 22 years and the homeowner is not happy! A tar epoxy style paint would have made a big difference. One such replacement paint is PPG's Sigmashield 880/Amerlock 880, a two-component, high-build, polyamine adduct-cured epoxy coating and is mentioned as a standard which should be met or exceeded by the paint you specify/use. To have given it a fighting chance the concrete should have

been 50 mm above the surrounding ground and sloped away from the post. As well, a lot of the posts used these days are duragal type product with a coating thickness of only 100 to 135 grammes per m2 where you should be aiming for 500. If you want to know more about the problems of steel posts I am sure David would be happy to talk to you and share his experience. His phone number is 1300 254 677

It is not all that difficult really. The image to the left is of some posts on a house my grandfather built over 100 years ago and are still going strong. They are de-sapped ironbark just put back in natural soil. Remember, concrete is your enemy with hardwood especially, as is not using durability one in ground timber. H5 treatment these days does away with the need to de-sap.

Report on Timber Queensland Seminar, February 25.

Timber Queensland held another CPD seminar on the 25th entitled *Design & Build: Timber Floors, Decks & Battens*. There were about 190 in attendance. I spoke on Battens, Colin Mckenzie on decks and Robert Clague of NS Timber Flooring spoke on, obviously, timber flooring. Timber Flooring has got a lot harder than it used to be when the timber was milled locally, dried locally and used locally. What was new ground for me was the presentation by Silvia Pugnaloni of Rotho Blaas Australia, an Italian manufacturer of specialty fixings and brackets. In my CPD session on timber joints I mention specialty concealed fixings that can be purchased in Europe. It was more of passing interest than of something that was going to have practical use due to availability. In Silvia's presentation she showed these brackets which are now available in Australia. It created a lot of interest. Here are some images. Her mobile is 0481 249 196.

If you are within easy travelling distance of Hamilton you really need a very good reason not to attend these meetings. Even an old hand like me came away with a better understanding. Here is the link to be on the mailing list for future events (see timber education alert).

Fencing Brackets (Not a paid advertisement)

I was about to hit the "publish" button on Amazon and finally put my timber fence book to bed when I thought I had better have another look for fence bracket suppliers in Australia. In the UK there is an embarrassment of riches in this field but I could find very little here. Lo and behold after several unsuccessful searches beforehand, this time I found a Brisbane company, Maclock, that makes a comprehensive range. I met with the owner, Barry McConnell and he advised me that some Bunnings stores are stocking them but their IT people should be congratulated on the completely successful way that they have hidden them on their website.

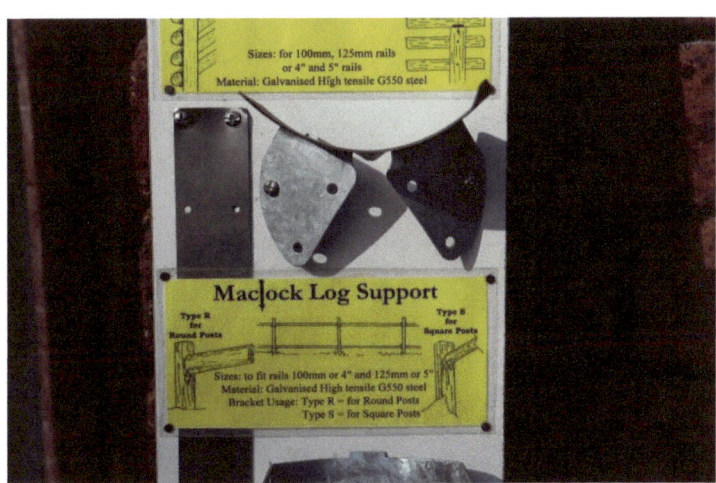
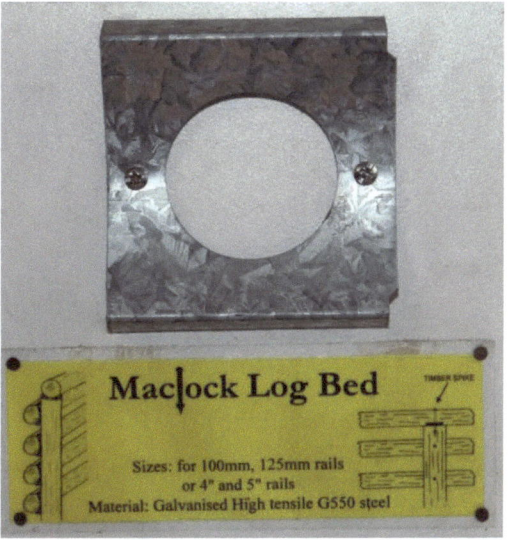

A good bracket can speed up construction considerably but remember that timber treatment manufacturers stipulate that they should be stainless within 8 k of the coast and hot dipped galvanised thereafter. Other nailplate manufacturers require all external plates to be stainless. Fortunately, these are available in 316 stainless. If stainless is unavailable a good heavy coat of a tar epoxy style paint would assist. The downside is ensuring contractors use the more expensive version. Barry can be contacted on 07 3390 8399.

.Timber Fence Book Finalised

The book on fencing, but for one image I cannot find, is complete. It covers hardwood, pine and cypress fences. Fences are a trap for architects and landscape architects as you are designing in an area where there are no standards, widespread ignorance among contractors (not my readers of course) and a huge variation of quality and performance. If you are a professional designer who has to provide certainty and repeatability in your fence designs, you need this book!

Do you like the fence on the front cover? It is a pity you have to go to Japan to find designers who appreciate the possibilities of spotted gum combined with customers who will pay for it. Image courtesy of Kurata Co. Go to http://www.ecowood.-or.jp/item/fence/index.html for more of their work. I would like to hear of good fence projects that can be added as case histories. What is next? Joints? I have also done a bit more on utilising small diameter hardwood.

What Do You Do With a Good Idea? (Not a paid commercial)

When I closed OSA back in 2012, I misplaced some of the documentation on the patents and registered design for Deckwood. Our Patent Attorney was able to help of course and incidentally it does not expire until 2019. My recent contact with the attorney and the fact that I have successfully marketed patents and received grants prompted me to share some practical advice with you on how to proceed with your great idea. So you have an idea on how to make a better widget, what do you do next.

You already have a gut feeling which is why you thought about it in the first place, and with the internet it is very easy. Consider
- is it novel
- if not entirely novel is it a significant improvement on what exists
- can enough widgets be sold to warrant the effort?:

Once you have satisfied yourself that you have something worth pursuing, initially a Patent Attorney would be engaged to undertake a preliminary novelty search costing about $1500. Once it has been established that there is no obvious prior art, you would then go to an Australian Patent Application which will give you a year's protection worldwide and cost about $5,000. This gives you a year to market the idea before patents have to be taken out overseas, which is where the large expenses are incurred. If your idea is not worth $6,500 it is probably not worth proceeding with. If the product can be licensed quickly, most of the future costs can even be deflected to the licensee before they are incurred. If you are only interested in the Australia market, you can bypass the application and go straight to an innovation patent but it only gives 8 years protection in a very small market. I have been very happy with my Patent Attorney, his details are:

My Patent Attorney is
Dr Ewen C Wynne
Wynnes Patent & Trademark Attorneys
P: +61 7 3399 4625, F: +61 7 3342 1292, E: ewynne@wynnes.com.au
WEB: www.wynnes.com.au
ADDRESS: Unit 4, 27 Godwin Street, Bulimba, Brisbane, QLD 4171

Before you get carried away spending money and time, you have to have in the forefront of your mind applying for grants. It is not that hard to get a grant and there are more now than when I used to apply. There is no single path to receiving a grant. There is a multiplicity of funds available; even from overseas though usually on a dollar for dollar basis and some will even backdate the research already done. Basically, any project with a "Wow Factor" can obtain a grant. From day one, have a notepad beside your desk and record every minute you think about it, every postage stamp, ever kilometre travelled and every "in kind" contribution. You will be shocked how quickly your expenses mount up. You need to plan your strategy for your grant early on and I would talk to a professional sooner rather than later. I used to do the applications myself but it is probably best to use a professional now. The person recommended by my Patent Attorney is:

John Dunleavy
Intertrade Advisors Pty Ltd,
P: 07 3238 8503, F: 07 3003 1863, M: 0412 077 311 E: john@intertrade.bz
ADDRESS: Unit 10, 913–915 Ann Street, Fortitude Valley Qld 4006

Don't think the world will beat a path to your door if you invent a better mousetrap. The hard work starts with marketing. Being an innovator can be a very frustrating and heartbreaking path to tread as you will find that people prefer the same old buggy whips grandfather used.

Edgar Stubbersfield

March 2016 Newsletter

A Reminder about Sleepers
How to Measure End Splits
World's Largest Timber Structure

A Reminder about Sleepers

I was out photographing a few jobs with a friend when he spotted, in the distance, what he thought was some of my work. On having a close look I was appalled at what was provided, installed and accepted. The barrier in the top two images are of that fence. Now, I do not know what was specified but I do know what was supplied - landscaping sleepers. This is a product that has no specification other than one reasonable edge and one reasonable face and it is arguable that what we see here even had that. The bottom two images of the four above are substandard sleepers substituted for my bollards.

The problem is that common sizes for landscaping, 200x50, 200x75 and 200x100 are also the sizes that landscaping sleepers are made in and they are probably a third of the price of structural timber of suitable quality. It is not surprising then that sleepers get used even often flaunting a reasonable specification. So how do you avoid this substitution? Well a suitable specification helps, here are two examples of specifications for bollards or fence posts:

125x125 or (200x100) spotted gum, ironbark or tallowwood, sapwood treated to H3 with ACQ or Tanalith E (CCA not acceptable) free of heart. Grade is Structural Grade 2 for all species. Inspect each piece to ensure defect is placed in ground. Mark base with lumber crayon before processing and make available for inspection prior to processing

NOTE: I do not recommend 200x75 or 150x150 for bollards - ask me why.

300x300 spotted gum, ironbark or tallowwood, sapwood treated to H3 with ACQ or Tanalith E (CCA not acceptable) . Grade is Structural Grade 2 for all species. Inspect each piece to ensure defect is placed in ground. Mark base with lumber crayon before processing and make available for inspection prior to processing. 300x300 is to have two expansion grooves per side which are to be formed within one week of milling.

NOTE: These species are automatically H5 if there is less than 20% sapwood which there will be.

The point is that the word "sleeper" should not be used by a design professional unless it is a recycled railway sleeper and then the grade has to be nominated.

How to Measure End Splits

The image to the left shows sleeper grade material used as rails and where the ends are badly split. So how do you assess end splits?

Firstly, to be officially called a "split", the split has to go from one face to another. If it is just on the one face it would be termed a check. The allowance for checks are so large you might as well ignore them when they are at the end.

But if the splits do go from one face to another the amount is limited from 100 to 150 mm depending on the grade. But that is the total aggregate of all the splits on one end. these pieces have up to six splits so at most they should be only 25mm long. Of course, when grading timber you have to use some common sense. If the timber has a 150mm split but you know you are going to trim it back 100 mm you would pass the timber as fit for purpose

World's Largest Timber Structure

There has been a lot of fanfare about the 10 story building built of cross laminated timber in Melbourne. While it is significant, it is not the height that is remarkable, it is the fact that it is a multi residential timber building without a sprinkler system that is remarkable. We have largely forgotten how over 70 years ago we were building massive timber structures. This section is a reminder of what we did.

So what is the largest timber structure? It all depends what criteria you use to define "largest" as to which one is the winner. Is it height, length, depth or volume. Some contenders are Metropol Parasol in Seville, Spain and the Daibutsu-den or Great Buddha Hall of the Todaiji Temple complex in the Nara, Japan. But as far as volume is concerned it would surely be the airship hangars built in the US during WW2.

A total of 17 airship hangars were built during the war, each hangar housed 8 airships that were 80 metres long. Because there was a steel shortage during the war, wood was chosen and the resulting hangars were reported to be the largest clear span timber structures built at that time. After the prototype was built, it only took a year to build the remaining seventeen, testimony to timbers versatility. The clear space inside the hangar at Tillamook (now an air museum) is span 90 metres, length 320 metres, and height 53 metres. The front doors are supported off 93m span timber box beams off 71m high concrete columns. The sister hanger to this at Tillamook was apparently completed in 27 working days.

How do you achieve such large spans? This is building on a scale several times larger than we saw in the ubiquitous WW2 aircraft hangars we used to see in around Australia.

The smaller Australian hangars were built from lineal 100x50 and simply nailed together yet the technology used in them was ground breaking and utilised timber up three times more efficiently than it had been before. The connections had to be much better.

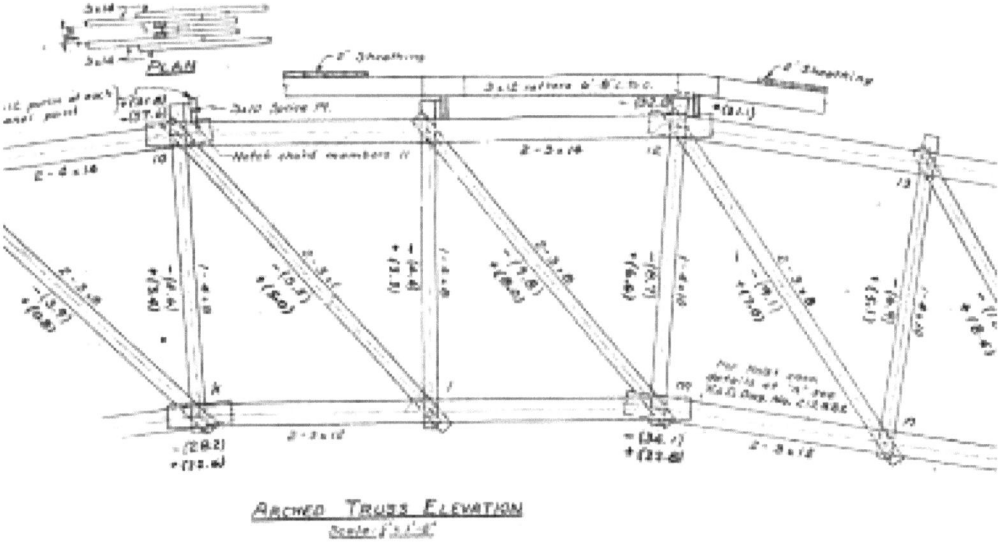

Figure 5. Detail of truss construction.
Source: Navy Department, Bureau Yards & Docks, Lighter-Than-Air Hangar Roof Truss Details, Drawing #212817, (August 5, 1942).

Structurally, the hangars feature 51 inverted catenary arch truss with a Pratt truss configuration with the truss frames at about 6 metre centres. The cords (double 350x75 for the top and double 300x75 for the bottom) are sawn oregon joined by steel split-ring connectors and bolts. There was 24,000 m3 of timber used at Tillamook, all of which was treated with fire-retardant salts (of dubious efficacy). Split rings have proved to be very efficient means of joining timbers.

Split rings are manufactured in imperial sizes in diameters of 63mm (2-1/2″) and 100mm (4″) from hot-rolled carbon steel for use with 13mm (1/2″) and 19mm (3/4″) diameter bolts respectively. A single split ring insets into both the precut grooves in the wood surface being joined. A tongue and groove split in the ring permits the ring to deform slightly under load so that all contact areas distribute load, and the special wedge shape on both sides of the ring eases insertion and ensures a tight fitting joint when the ring is fully seated in the grooves.

None of us are going to build an airship hangar so is there a use of split rings on smaller structures? The image above shows the rafters being attached to the posts in my office where they were connected with split rings. The rafters are 250 mm deep which means about 15 mm shrinkage overall. If you used two bolts the holes really should be elongated and that causes all manner of problems. But a single bolt with a split ring solved the shrinkage problem and gave a joint without any clearance. Note how I have used galvanised split rings. They are only black steel in Tillamook and are corroding but to be fair, it was only meant to be a temporary structure and never intended to end up on a register of heritage listed buildings.

I cannot see that these connectors are available in Australia any longer but they are readily available from the US and Canada

April 2016 - Special Edition

Large Timber Structures

I am hoping to write the normal monthly newsletter on Recycled timber which should come out later in the month but the opportunity has arisen to issue a special issue. When writing last month's newsletter on large timber structures, I remembered that a friend Dr. Dan Tingly told me that he had designed one of the world's largest timber structures. I asked him for some editorial and what he sent me was of such substance that it deserved a standalone newsletter. Dan's US company has conducted the survey on the Tillamook hangar below which we also saw last month. Either Dan or Bob Keller in his office designed a lot of the structures shown here. It would be a very foolish person that thought timber was yesterday's material.

If you want to know more about these buildings or large bridges contact Dan Tingly on Cell: 04 5957 6314 or 04 28983328 or email dant.tingley@gmail.com

LARGE BUILDINGS AND BRIDGES, SOME OLD SOME NEW!

Tillamook Blimp Hangar (now Tillamook Air Museum)

Tillamook Air Museum is an aviation museum south of Tillamook, Oregon, at Tillamook Airport in the

United States. The museum is housed in a former military blimp hangar, called "Hangar B", which is the largest clearspan solid sawn wooden structure in the world. Constructed by the US Navy in 1942 during World War II for Naval Air Station Tillamook, the hangar building housing the aircraft is 1,072 feet (327 m) long and 296 feet (90 m) wide, giving it over 7 acres (2.8 ha) of area. It stands at 192 feet (59 m) tall.

Belledune and Superior Dome Buildings

The Superior Dome, shown in the right hand photos, opened as the "world's largest wooden dome" on September 14, 1991, is a domed stadium on the campus of Northern Michigan University in Marquette, Michigan, in the United States. It is home to the Northern Michigan Wildcats football team, as well as a variety of campus and community events. The dome is 14 stories tall, has a diameter of 536 feet (163 m), and covers an area of 5.1 acres (21,000 m2). It is a geodesic dome constructed with 781 Douglas Fir beams and 108.5 miles (174.6 km) of fir decking. The Belledune Coal storage building is located in Belledune, New Brunswick, Canada.

Edgar Stubbersfield

Hokkaido Bridge

Hokkaido Bridge Japan is a 38m clear span two lane highway bridge including trucks. HS 20 rated. Called "Bridge of a Thousand Trees", it has 1m deep beams due to a waterway restriction needing clear height. The spacing of the girders was 4 foot on center and they were reinforced with high strength fiber. Mitsubishi was the contractor. The bridge had a glulam vertical lam deck and a wood rail system. It was shipped in short length components and fixed end moment connectors were used to make long span girders for installation on site.

Hartland Covered Bridge

The **Hartland Bridge** in Hartland, New Brunswick, is the world's longest covered bridge, at 1,282 feet (391 m) long. It crosses the Saint John River from Hartland to Somerville, New Brunswick, Canada. The framework consists of seven small Howe Truss bridges joined together on six piers. Plans and specifications of the bridge began in 1898 and the bridge was constructed in 1901 by the Hartland Bridge Company.

Large Timber Bridges (other)

The **Lower Burnett Road Bridge** is a three-span, timber arch bridge in Buckley, Washington. The bridge is located in the middle of a switchback where the old railroad grade gained 60.96m (200 ft) in a little more than 3.2 km (2 miles), with a horizontal radius of 198m (650'-0"). The bridge spans South Prairie Creek and Lower Burnett Road with a total span of 118.86m (389'-11½"). The structure is 5.49m (18'-0") wide and is designed to carry H15 vehicle loading in addition to the 4.07kPa (85 psf) pedestrian load

The **Bow Bridge** on Big Wood River _ Draper, ID - 160' x 6' Pinned Arch Timber Bridge, which crosses the Big Wood River at the Draper Preserve in Hailey. The Bow Bridge of the Big Wood River was designed to mimic a recurve bow that appears to have been dropped from the sky, landing string side down. The bridge now connects the East and West banks of the Big Wood.

The **Whistlestop Forest Service Bridge** in the Chugach National Forest on Alaska's Kenai Peninsula. At 280 feet, this camel back truss structure is the longest clear-span timber bridge in the US. The bridge is 14'-10 ¾" wide with a 6'-0" wide walkway. The top of the bridge to the water level is approximately 50 feet with 20 feet of clearance from the water and about 30 feet of total bridge height in the center of the span. The bridge was designed with enough clearance to ensure that any ice bergs coming down stream during periods of high flow would pass freely under the bridge. Douglas fir glulam treated with pentachlorophenol preservative was used for the truss members, floor beams, purlins, and all bracing members. The 280-foot trusses are 15-feet high at the ends and more than 27-feet high at midspan. The structure rests on steel H-piles driven about 40 feet into the ground at the east and west ends.

The entrance to **Overpeck Park** in Bergen County, New Jersey, lies immediately adjacent to the interchange of the Interstate 80 and Interstate 95 freeways. The county, recognizing that thousands of commuters would see this entrance structure daily, chose identical glulam arch bridges for this entrance structure. Each bridge is a 42.67m (140'-0") tied arch bridge with a 9.14m (30'-0") roadway and a 3.05m (10'-0") walkway on one side only.

Unusual Timber Bridges

In the depths of northeastern India, in one of the wettest places on earth, bridges aren't built - they're grown. The living bridges of Cherrapunji, India are made from the roots of the Ficus elastica tree. This tree produces a series of secondary roots from higher up its trunk and can comfortably perch atop huge boulders along the riverbanks, or even in the middle of the rivers themselves. The root bridges, some of which are over a hundred feet long, take ten to fifteen years to become fully functional, but they're extraordinarily strong - strong enough that some of them can support the weight of fifty or more people at a time. Because they are alive and still growing, the bridges actually gain strength over time - and some of the ancient root bridges used daily by the people of the villages around Cherrapunji may be well over five hundred years old.

Edgar Stubbersfield

April 2016

Recycled Timber - Political Correctness?
Large Timber Structure Follow up
Everything Fencing

Recycled Timber - Political Correctness?

I am afraid I have been around for too long because I am getting cynical in my old age, especially when it comes to fashions in timber specification. Take treated pine, we went through a period when political correctness drove the specification of treated pine for boardwalks in Queensland. But being politically correct did not make it correct and now the large majority of these have been replaced with hardwood. Now as an example of political correctness in specifying, we are seeing plastic decking used in commercial applications, a practice, to me, is beyond comprehension and also specifying recycled timber as a throwaway line without working through the issues of such a request.

Don't misunderstand me, there is certainly a place for recycled timber. Consider the image above (courtesy of Guymer Bailey Architects) where the recycled timber isn't really doing anything structural and for what it is doing it is well oversized. You could look at this and quite rightly have a case of the warm and fuzzies, which of course it was intended to do and does so very successfully. But while some timber applications just have to look good, other timber has to perform well and/or have very different aesthetic requirements.

The poor owner of a home in residential subdivision in Brisbane had a rude shock when his timber driveway failed. It was built from recycled timber and would have been very expensive but the timber was worn out before a single tyre passed over it. A situation like this needs the performance, species and grades that we associate with new timber. It will involve limiting the amount of heart in sawn members.

The bollard on the left has a starburst split (remember how much end split you can have from last month's newsletter) and so is of an unacceptable quality for sale as new timber. Despite this someone probably paid twice the going rate for this piece compared with new high quality timber. Now, the heart could easily have been tamed with expansion grooves. The bollard on the right is new timber supplied and processed by me. Its relevance to the discussion is that it was the reply to a call for help. The original material chosen for this project was recycled Durability 1 hardwood. It was supplied in turpentine (old marine piles) and in a couple of months had shrunk 10% and was of extremely poor quality. The expansion joint is on the water side. Regrettably there is no image of the offending material. Remember, if it is cut from a round piece it is going to behave like unseasoned timber because the original piece was too large to season.

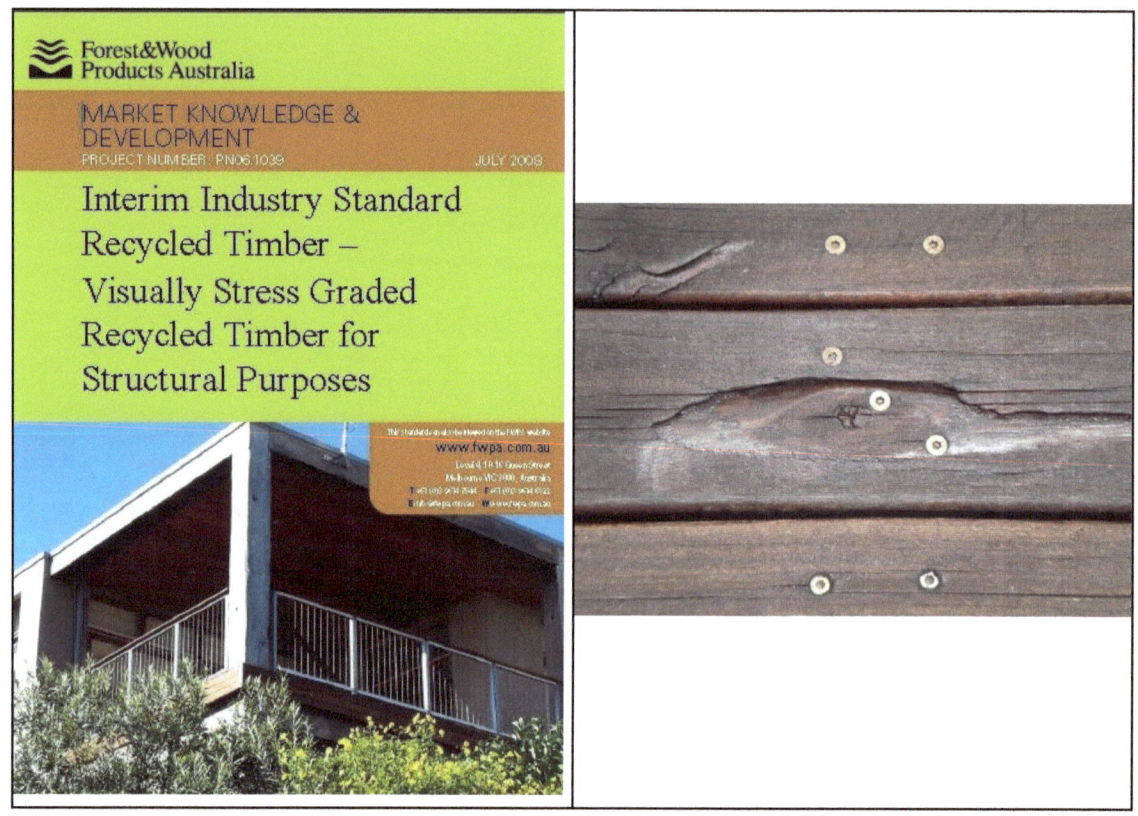

There is a standard for recycled structural timber which is suitable for the types of applications that it illustrates, oversize decorative conversation pieces having some structural load However you need to keep in mind that the standards for visually grading sawn hardwood and pine recognize four different grades, the structural recycled standard only recognizes two grades - Recycled Grade 1 and Recycled Grade 2. The better grade, Recycled Grade 1, is basically the same as Structural Grade 2 in AS2082 (or 60% of the strength of defect free timber). This is too low a grade for decking and external battens and cannot give you the required high quality weather resisting face and edge. This is particularly the case with smaller pieces. Take the piece of recycled decking on the right, that defect will slice a foot open. No amount of green points can make up for the injury this can cause.

Things like decking and architectural battens need a specification no less demanding than that of new timber. For example, a specification for a recycled batten should be as follows - the top and weather side should be graded to Structural Grade One; the back and bottom should be graded to a minimum of Structural Grade 2. This is irrespective of species. So use recycled by all means but please be aware of the intricacy involved and do not be persuaded by slick talking salesmen.

Large Timber Structures Followup

There was a lot of positive feedback about the two newsletters on large timber structures. Did you miss them? Here are the links - see March Newsletter April Special Edition. What created the most interest was the Tillamook blimp hangar covering 7 acres. I found the plans to a sister hangar in the library of congress. It is worth a look. If you are still of the view that timber is yesterday's material look at the proposed timber skyscraper for London. Will it get built, probably not, but the point is that while we are agonising about eight story buildings here in Australia, people overseas are already thinking of 80 story buildings!

Everything Fencing

I received some images of two very amazing fences built by our Japanese friends at Kurata Co using spotted gum. I have included two of them above. This is how good fencing and workmanship can be. I have used another of their fences as a case history in my fencing book. Now I am supposing you are thinking, what do I need a book on fencing for, why do I need to spend $33? Compare this fence to the case history of an Australian Residential estate in the fence book.. It is money well spent just to get a material specification.

On the subject of fences, we had a wind storm pass through a narrow area of my Lockyer Valley a few weeks back and fences were very badly hit, particularly the Colorbond style ones. Some timber fences did not fare very well either, particularly when the rails were checked into the posts for the full depth. Checking posts into rails is such common practice that I can't imagine we will ever be able to stop it but on these large blocks it is a pointless exercise trying to economise on space. Just screwing the rails to the post would be a much better option especially with stainless batten screws.

May 2016

Coming Soon - My New Book on Timber Joints
Non Durable Timber has Lasted Over 100 Years Outside
Timber Bollards That Have Not Aged Gracefully
The State of Timber Research in Australia

Coming Soon - My New Book on Timber Joints.

Tamedia building in Switzerland - Images courtesy of Eileen Newbury, FWPA

The Tamedia building in Switzerland by Shigeru Ban Architects in Japan clearly demonstrates that here in Australia we are only paddling around the edges of what is possible with timber - visit the Tamedia website for more images. The images of the joints in the Tamedia building shows that there is potentially no limit when discussing timber joints. I have finished the chapters on split rings and shear plates and the relationship of F grads to joint group so far. Split rings and shear plates, which are still common in the US, are very important in the scheme of things as they allowed reliable design of joints for the first time.

I would love any images you have of joints and suggestions for content.

Non Durable Timber Has Lasted More Than 100 years

The heritage listed headrig from the Sons of Gwalia mine in WA utilising 300x300 Oregon pine was constructed between 1896-8, so it is roughly 120 years old. It was built by the mining engineer Herbert Hoover who went on to great fame but not by inventing the vacuum cleaner but instead by becoming the 31st president of the US. He protected the headrig from termite attack but could not protect it from the weather and being Oregon you would have expected it last one tenth the time that it has. About one third has been replaced with karri which is not a vast improvement on Oregon (Durability 3 in ground) but otherwise it is still sound. The secret is the very dry environment (see the November 2015 Newsletter also). Sons of Gwalia? The original backer of the project was Welch and Gwalia is an old name for Wales. My advice has been to design as if you are in a harsh environment and it will reward you in a less demanding climate.

Timber Bollards That Have Not aged Gracefully

I covered how to make a success of sawn timber bollards in my October 2015 newsletter now it is time to look at natural rounds. If you have done my CPD session on using "heart in" hardwood you would have seen the image in the top slide which I took in 2005. (If you haven't done it, why not?) This slide is used to show how not to use heart in timber. The natural rounds are Ironbark and someone would have looked up a book and saw that it was Durability Class 1 and thought it was a good idea to use them. "Be there for 50 years", was probably the thought. But the durability rating refers to heartwood and untreated sapwood is always durability 4. That means the sapwood of ironbark is basically the same durability as the sapwood of pine. Now, 11 years later they are in a very sad state, as indeed they had to be. You can see from the loose ring on the bollard on the lower left hand image just how much of the cross section has been lost as the sapwood decayed.

The other issues I highlighted with the bollard were the sharp corners on the strap, hopelessly light screws on the saddles (since replaced) and no protection of the heart. What was not evident when new was that the bollards were not installed deep enough. They only went in 450 mm whereas 600 mm should be the minimum. Many have a considerable lean because of this. Now, what is left of these bollards will probably last another 20 years but they look so frightful that many have already been replaced. Tragically the asset owner has used plastic which, in my opinion, is an even worse solution. I will bring you a image when as I expect, someone with a bull bar on his 4WD mows over 50 of them in one hit.

The best thing that a designer can have is a supplier that will say to you, "Please don't do this" but they are few and far between. Conversely. a responsible supplier has to find someone who will listen. Think how many thousands of dollars could have been saved by engaging me for just one hour. It wasn't hard to make them a success. These natural round bollards were supplied by me in the late 70's or very early 80's. They are treated so the sapwood has not decayed.

These bollards are not capped and it is only when they get some age on them that the need for caps becomes obvious. The band of treated sapwood is in good shape but the centre, which will not accept treatment is deteriorating.

This row of treated sawn bollards is literally just around the corner from the untreated rounds. They are as good as the bollards we produced. It is not hard to get it right but it is not hard to get it entirely wrong also. The bollards in the October 2015 newsletter have the same asset owner as these.

Timber Newsletters 2014-2017

The State of Timber Research in Australia
Part 1 of 2

Edgar Stubbersfield

Views from the Salisbury Research Facilities of Agri-Science Queensland

The strength in forest product research in Australia can be summarised in one word, "Queensland". Forgive me a brief quote from Hansard "In the early 1950s, some of the great inventions of the world—the hi-fi, the colour photocopier or whatever—were all invented here, in Australia. In fact, one of the scientists was a guy called Alwyn Clements, who lived in my electorate. He was a very smart man. Did we develop those inventions? No. Under the years of Menzies, all those sorts of things went offshore. Menzies was supposed to have said to Clements, `Your transistor will never replace the valve". We have done it yet again, this time with timber.

Dr Henri Bailleres heads up the Forest Product Innovation Team, a team of enthusiastic scientists, technicians and operational staff at Australia's only dedicated forest product research facilities, the Salisbury Research Facility, The team and facility sit under the banner of the Queensland Government's Department of Agriculture and Fisheries. This research team and facility combine enabling research and development activities for direct benefit to the forest, forest products and construction industries. The team have comprehensive skills and experience in forest resource assessments, processing and seasoning systems, engineered wood product design and prototyping, performance assessments, adhesives/adhesion development and protection systems.

This research facility is not just boffins in lab coats, and they have these, but it incorporates semi industrial scale processing equipment (more on this next month). The work being carried out at Salisbury is amazing. Here are some instances:

Henri is holding a piece of timber joined with nail plates ready to be tested to destruction. In my research for the book on joints I have been looking at nail plates. Originally they had short teeth and were held in by ancillary nailing, then the breakthrough was straight but longer teeth and through constant innovation and testing the tooth design, depth and layout has evolved and is still evolving, The Salisbury Research Facility has some sophisticated equipment that allows it to further improve the performance of a range of timber jointing systems.

This sheet is an original attempt to produce a prototype building panel manufactured from agri-fibre, in this case sorghum stalks. Similar experiments with sugarcane bagasse performed by FPI crew showed boards could be produced with better properties than standard particleboard. Utilisation of these by-product fibres could become very important in the future.

The Salisbury people have demonstrated that plantations originally intended for loo rolls will give a better return as veneer-based engineered wood products such as plywood. They have introduced spindleless veneer lathe technology to Australia and used this relatively low-cost processing technology to recover valuable wood at rates many times higher than achieved using conventional processing approaches such as sawmilling. Their research has demonstrated that much higher value can be recovered from young fast growing hardwoods.

.Engineered Wood Products (EWPs) are where a lot of effort has been placed. For example, until now, developing adhesive systems and the manufacturing protocols for products like plywood has been a time consuming process where panels are made and then split with chisels to see how good the adhesion was. Henri has taken a scientific approach. An Automatic Bonding Evaluation System (ABES) enables the team to fast-track this process. The ABES can control the temperature, pressure and time on small specimens with which the two veneers are joined, as well as the climatic conditions. It will then measure in one operation the force that is needed for the bond to break, all within a few minutes. This system provides a very fast way to determine the optimum parameters for high quality adhesion. If you have a timber related research question you may wish to contact Henri. His details are:

Henri BAILLERES, B App Sci (forestry), M eng (wood Sci and Tec), PhD
Team leader Forest Products Innovation
Horticulture & Forestry Science
Agri-Science Queensland
Department of Agriculture and Fisheries
50 Evans Rd, Salisbury 4107 QLD Australia
Telephone + 61 (0)7 3272 9327
Facsimile + 61 (0)7 3875 1015Mobile + 61 (0)4 3460 6524
Website: https://www.daff.qld.gov.au/forestry/research-and- innovation

June 2016

Galvanised Bolts More Variable Than Steel
The State of Timber Research In Australia
Contribution to French Book on Tropical Timber
Problems Looming with Self Drilling Screws
An Accountant That Helped Me
The Largest Timber Church in Australia

Galvanised Bolts More Variable Than Timber

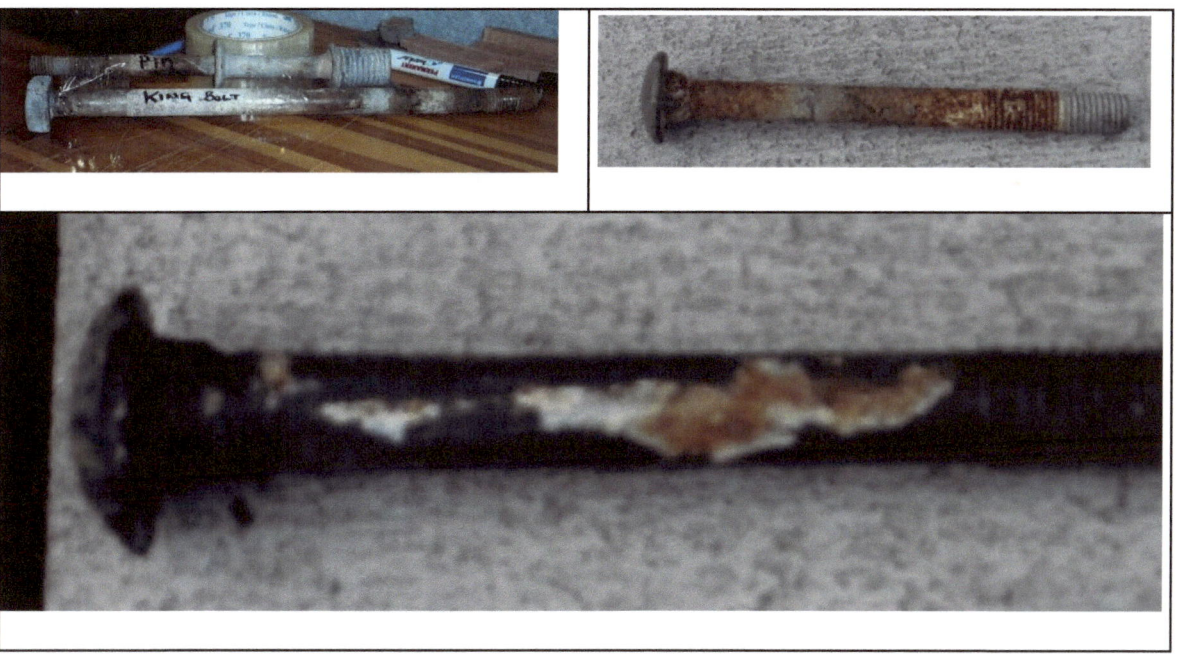

The image on the top left hand is of an Australian made bolt installed on a cross arm on a powerpole at Millmerran in 1950 and removed in 2001 and which, after 50 years, still has some galvanising in place, The image on the top right is of an imported bolt after 12 months in Gatton, a very similar environment. The galvanising has completely failed,

The lower image is of a bolt painted with a suitable epoxy and removed after three months. The galvanising has separated from the steel taking the paint with it. When I saw this bolt I took some of the same batch to a laboratory to tell me what was happening. They looked at the bolt and said, "Look how shiny it is. It must be electroplated, but we will check it to be sure." They rang back to say that they were indeed hot dipped galvanised and according to the relevant standard were very well galvanised. They further commented that obviously it was not working and could not offer a suggestion why. Because of this I have always, in my CPD sessions, advised professionals to specify stainless bolts because it left us as a supplier with a real quandary as I would never sell anything if I priced with the more expensive fastener.

Is this extremist? I do not think so, even if you consider a well galvanised bolt. Bolts are galvanised in small batches in wire cages which are then spun at high revolutions to remove excess zinc and give a clean thread. The typical minimum coating thickness for a 10 mm bolt or larger would be 390 g/m^2 or 55 microns. By contrast, the minimum coated thickness for steel over 6 mm, which sits in the vat for up to 10 minutes is 600 g/m^2 or 85 microns and regularly reaches 700-900 g/m^2. Longevity is dependent on the zinc coating so normal steel could have an expected life of 30 to 50% longer than that of the bolt

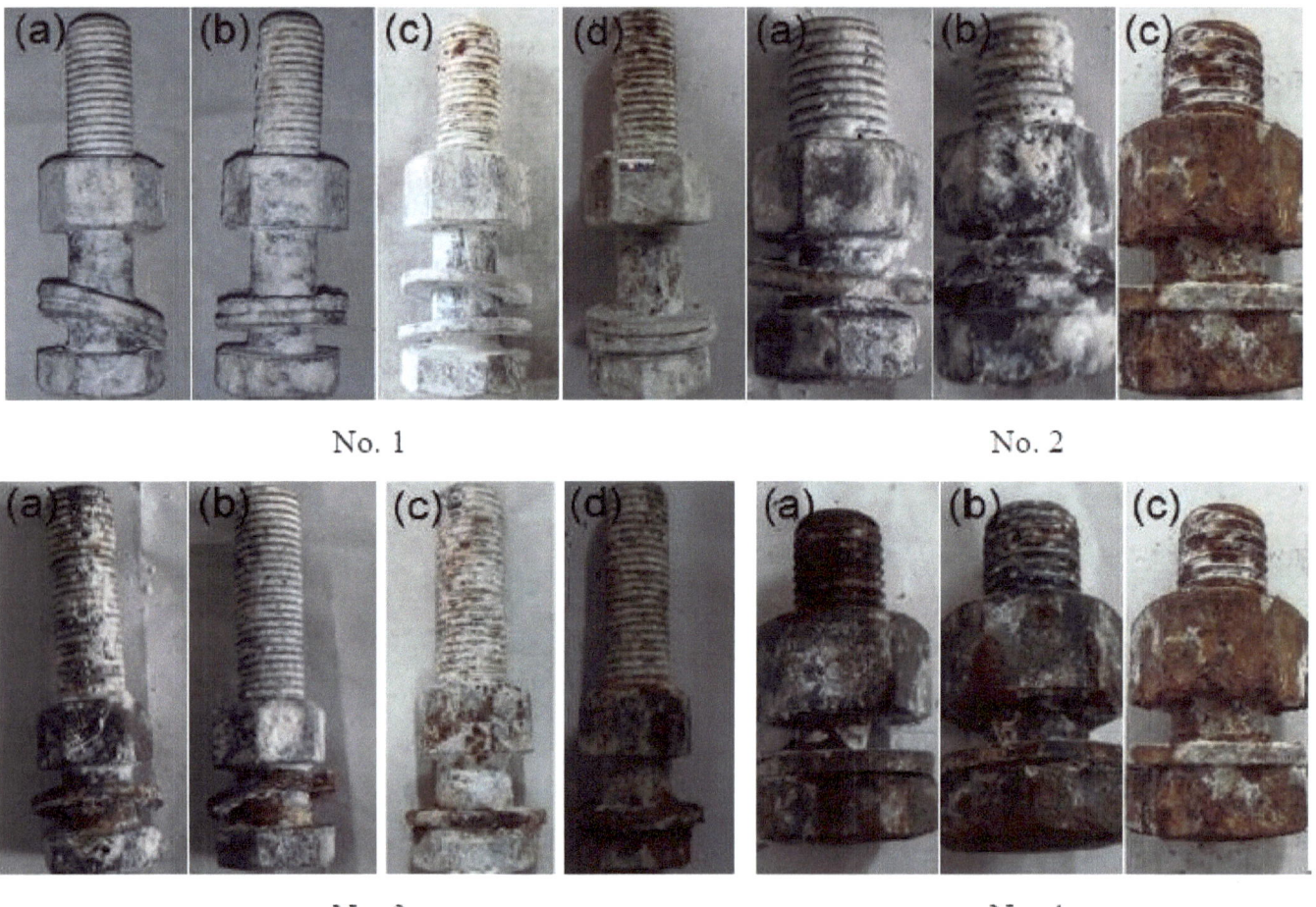

Fig. 1 Corrosion photos of No. 1 ~ No. 4 in neutral salt fog environment
(a) 500 h; (b) 1000 h; (c) 1500 h; (d) 3000 h

Until now, I have not been able to get publically available information on how bad the imported bolts can be. It was as if there was a conspiracy of silence. An article written in the Journal of Applied Mechanics and Materials on the anti-corrosion performance of four randomly purchased bolts in China identified the problem and more importantly offered suggestions as to why. The conclusion was *"The anti-corrosion performance of the four hot-dip galvanizing bolts obtained from different company were all unsatisfactory. The causes of the above phenomenon are the lower thickness of the hot-dip coating, too much defects on the surface of the coatings and the elemental composition impurity".*

How great was the variability of the galvanising? the average coating thickness on individual bolts went from 130 um to 34 um and the minimum was 13 um which happened to be on the same bolt that averaged 130 um. This is greater variability than timber and can mean that the bolt, not the timber, is the weak link in the system.

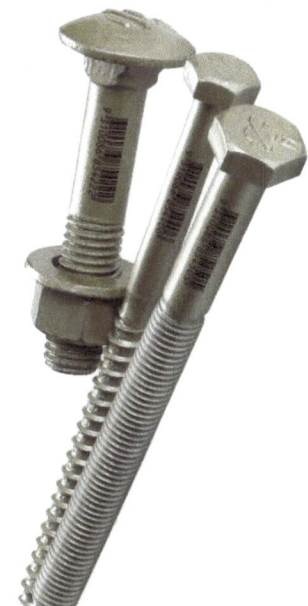

Is there an alternative to stainless steel? Quite possibly and that is ITW Prolines Tech-Shield™ coated bolts. This is an epoxy coating applied with an electric charge which endures an even coating. ITW is the only Australian organisation I am aware of which has taken the issue of poor performance of imported galvanised bolts very seriously. In conjunction with ITW technical coating specialists in Asia and the United States, they developed a new advanced barrier coating that helps bolts fight off the chemicals found in treated timber. This ultimately extends the life of the bolt. Apparently when tested at an Independent laboratory to international and Australian standards Tech-Shield™ provided, on average, 3.9 times the protection of their regular hot dipped galvanised bolts when used in treated pine. Unfortunately they were not available when I operated my business so I don't have personal experience but the company has considerable credibility with me and this isn't a paid advertisement.

To determine the suitability of this product for your needs contact David Collinson at ITW. His email is david.collinson@itwcap.com

Note: The journal article is Li. Cuoxin, Shanjing Xia, Yilang Peng. Anti-Corrosion Performance of Four Hot Dip Galvanising Bolts in *Applied Mechanics and Materials Vols. 395-396* (2013) pp 708-711

The State of Timber Research in Australia
Part 2 of 2

This section is postponed as there is some important news to relate next month.

Published in Memento Du Forestier Tropical

In conjunction with Henri Bailleres (on the right) Team Leader, Forest Products Innovation and Gary Hopewell Senior Research Scientist, Horticulture and Forestry Science (obviously then on the left) of the Department of Agriculture and Fisheries, I contributed a chapter on timber construction to the prestigious French publication *Memento du Forestier Tropical.* Despite being a 1200 page book, we were all a little miffed at the way our document had been trimmed for publication until we saw the USB stick attached where the expanded document can be found along with 1000 colour images! A more recent example of cutting edge technology again from the French! Read French, ask me for a copy of the article.

Problems looming with self drilling screws

When the Tek patent expired, the Australian market was flooded with low cost, low quality lookalikes. The protective coating could be down to 2-3 microns of electroplated zinc giving only 25% of the corrosion protection of the original ITW Buildex product The implications for corrosion in any timber, let alone treated timber, through inadvertently using poor quality coatings, is obvious. The demand of roofing manufacturers in 1981 that their screws be able to withstand 1000 hours of the standard salt spray test led eventually to AS 3566 – Self Drilling Screws. This Standard was unusual as it is a performance based specification and not a materials specification. Regrettably, this very good standard was withdrawn in 2015.

I understand that large purchasers of screws are still requiring compliance with the old standard and you would be wise to insist on it also, But in practical terms, unless human nature has changed, what brand of screw you use now will depend on how much you trust the manufacturer's guarantee.

Largest Timber Church in Australia

Travelling from my home in Gatton through Rosewood on the way to Ipswich in Queensland you go past the interesting old Rising Sun Hotel. No doubt, it has been the ruin of many a poor boy just like its namesake in New Orleans. But, if you turn to your left before you cross the railway line you will find St Bridget's Catholic Church which we can only hope has been the redemption of some. If you love timber, you will love this 1910 building which claims (as a few others do) to be the biggest timber church in the country. Here are a few images to ponder how things used to be done.

The only timbers I could identify were floor which is crows ash and the pews which are hoop pine. Even the altar and the handrails are timber, a testimony to the decorators skill to make it look like marble. The pressed metal ceiling is brilliant. A special thanks to St. Bridget's parish for opening the church so I could bring you these images.

Edgar Stubbersfield

July 2016

What Brand Paint should I Use?
More on Galvanised Bolts
Designing, Specifying & Building Timber Structures: An Induction Workshop
The State of Timber Research in Australia
Concrete Sleepers or Timber

What Brand Paint Should I Use?

I have just had the timber handrails on my home painted and, as you can see, they were labour intensive so the correct choice of paint was critically important. But then the same problem is faced by all my readers as there are serious consequences if you get it wrong. We are all too aware that paint quality, like paint prices, vary considerably and once you have experienced what life has to offer you should become sceptical about linking price and quality. At the same time you may have become wary about thinking that slick advertising also means top quality. So how do you decide what brand to specify or use when you do not have the specialist knowledge to assess quite complex chemistry?

Fortunately the Australian Paint Accreditation Scheme (APAS) is at your rescue. Australia has the largest paint accreditation schemes in the world and it is run by the CSIRO, arguably our most trusted scientific body. APAS was initially set up by the state governments and different federal agencies as they have a vested interest in ensuring long lived material is used. The CSIRO (in effect) has written the specification and they have tested the paints independently and accredited them and the associated manufacturing facilities. For a paint to get the APAS tick of approval it must exceed the specification. On the APAS website you can find the list of participating manufacturers. If the paint meets the specification it can be used with confidence and price is not important. Ensure the paint you use has the APAS logo.

More on Galvanised Bolts

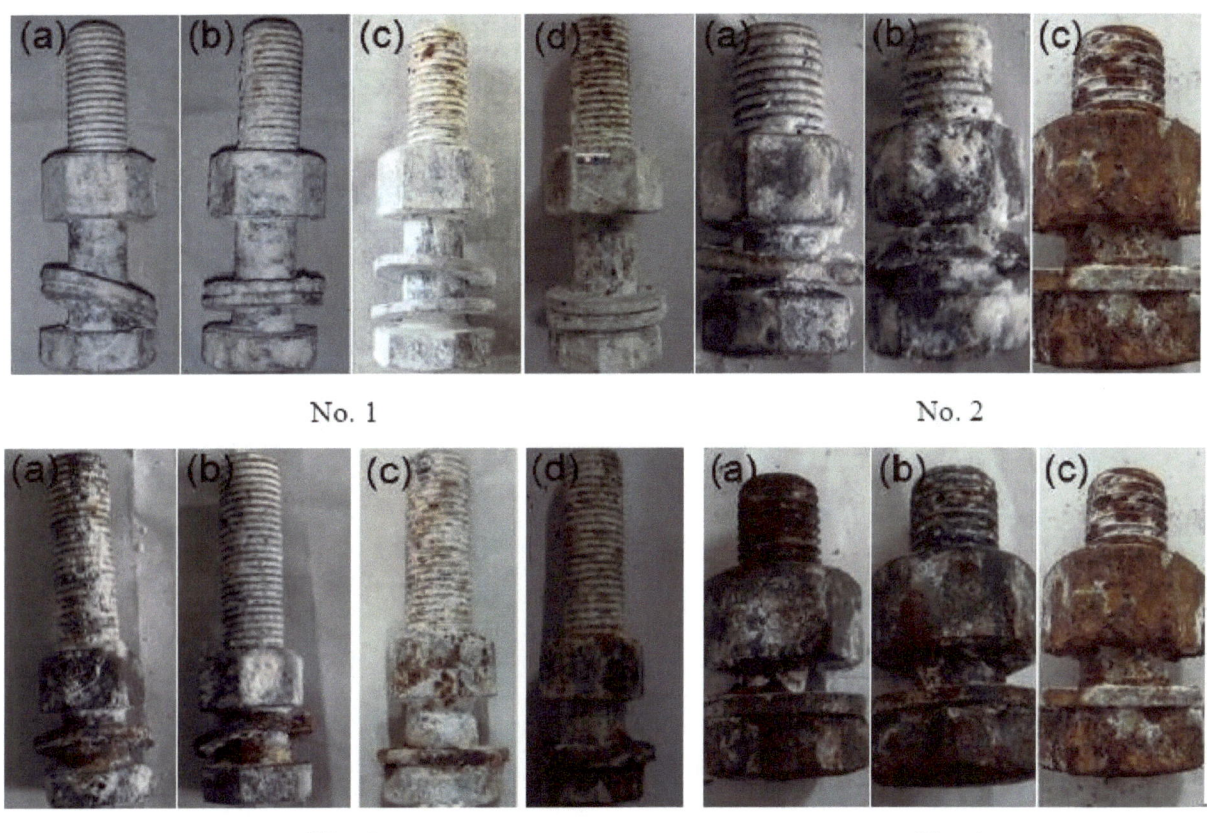

Fig. 1 Corrosion photos of No. 1 ~ No. 4 in neutral salt fog environment
(a) 500 h; (b) 1000 h; (c) 1500 h; (d) 3000 h

Last month I had a section stating that imported galvanised bolts can be more variable than the timber they were connecting. I had excellent feedback from one of my readers who is the Principal Consultant - Coatings & Advanced Materials for a very respected firm of engineers. His detailed reply concluded, "It is my firm belief that galvanised fasteners are only suitable for timber constructions if the conditions are and continue to be ideal. Due the unpredictability and number of variables that influence exposure conditions as well as the substrate, selecting more corrosion resistant fasteners significantly reduces the risk of premature corrosion."

A useful resource to assist you in understanding whether to use galvanised fasteners or not is Corrosion of Metals in Wood Products by Dr. Samuel Zelinka. What I found particularly helpful was Section Six which deals with the difference between atmospheric corrosion of a galvanised finish and corrosion in wood. In his conclusion he says, "Corrosion in wood is not atmospheric corrosion. Corrosion in wood is different from atmospheric corrosion. There are different thermodynamics, different kinetics, and different corrosion products form. It is not safe to assume that just because a solution works for atmospheric corrosion that it is a good idea to apply it to fastener corrosion in wood." Dr Zelinka is the Project Leader, Building and Fire Sciences, Forest Products Laboratory, USDA Forest Service and has written many useful documents on the subject of corrosion.

Of course, corrosion is not an issue in a non ventilated roof with nail plated trusses as the moisture content quickly drops below 20%. Historically, away from the coast, black steel bolts have done well in this situation. Once we talk weather exposed structures, that is a totally different situation as once we have moisture we have the potential for corrosion.

The State of Timber Research in Australia
Part 2 of 2
Centre for Future Timber Structures research centre at the University of Queensland

From right to left: Dr Rob McGavin, Forestry Minister Leanne Donaldson and Dr Henri Bailleres. Image by James Bowden from TIMBER&FORESTRY ENEWS

Despite wood being an ideal construction material with significant environmental and economic advantages over concrete and steel, Australian construction authorities were cautious about its use in multi story buildings. This has caused Australia to lag behind other developed countries in the adoption of tall timber buildings. While the National Construction Code now allows builders to use timber for buildings up to 25 metres in height – or around 8 storeys, the technology to make this commonplace, particularly in tropical and subtropical areas, is still in its infancy.

In May, the Federal Government announced $4 million in new funding toward the establishment of a National Institute for Forest Products Innovation but its two key centres will be located in Tasmania and South Australia. This Federal initiative ignored the existing world class R&D capability in Queensland. There are a number of centres around the world working on this same idea and, and like the proposed new centres, they are all in milder climates. It made sense to have a third centre in Queensland which offers the opportunity to develop the use of timber in commercial buildings in sub-tropical and tropical climates.

Researchers from the Department of Agriculture and Fisheries Forest Product Innovation team at the Salisbury research facility have been instrumental in establishing the Centre for Future Timber Structures research centre at the University of Queensland which was opened this month. They will work closely with scientists from UQ and elsewhere to ensure the success of the centres mission. This mission "is to engineer new timber building products, deliver tall timber buildings and transform Queensland's timber industry in the process." The researchers plan to develop products using techniques from the aerospace industry to greatly improve the strength of timber products. Already work is underway on the use of robotic construction to dramatically increase construction speed, reduce weight and cut waste on site. Fire, of course, is the obvious objection so specialists in this field will work closely with Queensland Fire and Emergency Service to ensure the inherent fire safety of timber products and construction.

This has all required new money which has come from the Queensland Government which invested $1 million which in turn has been matched by the University of Queensland. The Australian Research Council is providing an additional $1.5 million to the project. Private sector partners are Queensland-based timber processor Hyne Timber, global engineering firm Arup Engineering and the major building company Lendlease. Lendlease has already constructed high-rise timber buildings in Melbourne. All up this funding matches the federal government's contribution to the southern centres. For more information contact Dr Bailleres.

Concrete Sleepers or Timber?

A new motel is being built next door to my home, a little tedious but nothing I can do about it. There are a number of expensive retaining walls being built using galvanised steel posts and coloured textured concrete sleepers. Quite frankly I believe this is a better option than using most of the treated pine landscaping on the market. Sadly it need not be the case. Let me explain...

The spacing they have used of 2.4 metres would have required an F7 200x100 pine sleeper. This size sleeper wholesales for about $400 m3 (abt. $19.20 each) and would sell at trade at the big boxes for about $475 m3 (abt. $22.8 each) but they are not structurally rated! So, if you value your professional indemnity, you simply cannot use them. Next there is a high probability they are not treated well – refer to the January newsletter. Now, the suppliers could guarantee penetration of the preservative into the heartwood by incising (see images above). This process is seen as a cost of doing business on the west cost of the USA and increasingly in the UK. The cost to do this in the

Incised post - Image courtesy of Walford Timber Limited and Koppers Performance Chemicals

Excalibur Incising machine for round timber - Image courtesy of Arch Timber Protection - a member of the UK Timber Decking and Cladding Association

production line is probably about $25 per m3 or $1.20 each. So a sleeper that has the improved durability, and allowing some profit on the incising, is about $24.50 - $25.00 each but it is still not structurally rated! Let's assume then that behind the inciser you put a proof grader and you have 10% loss of timber not meeting specification, you now have a product getting close to being fit for use and it is under $30. But at this stage it is all hypothetical as, to my knowledge, such a product does not exist on the Australian market. And that is not factoring in the extra cost of treating to H5 instead of H4 which in ACQ will probably add another $7-8 each per sleeper at trade. If we go to concrete we will need two sleepers (from the one company I approached) to do the same job of one piece of pine. That will sell at trade for about $70.

So until some smart timber manufacturer sees the opportunity and runs with it, I am loathed to say, in my opinion you are better off with concrete. As for incising, keep insisting on it for any external pine application. I am told that there is starting to be interest by millers in installing in- line incising plants. There are only two of these plants in the country at the moment, but as there are two manufacturers it cannot be said that it is not available.

Edgar Stubbersfield

August 2016

Tamedia Building, Zurich
Revised Standard AS/NZS 1170.2 Released
The Two Henry Fords of Housing
They Are Not Using Shipping Containers Are They?

Tamedia Building, Zurich

© Blumer-Lehmann AG, 9200 Gossau / Abdruck mit Quellenangabe erlaubt

The Tamedia building in Zurich by architect Shigeru Ban graphically illustrates how inexhaustible the subject of timber joints is. I have included a case history of the building and more images in the joints book. (Readers should contact me direct for that free chapter).

Image copyright Tamedia and used with permission.

Revised Standard AS/NZS 1170.2 Released

The fourth amendment to AS/NZS 1170.2 Structural design actions - Wind actions has now been published There are some very serious changes.

The Two Henry Fords of Housing
Part 1 of 2

Researching my new book on timber joints I came across two men, William Levitt and John Calvin Jureit who would both be likened to Henry Ford in the way they transformed housing from being crafted one at a time into an assembly line construction that we are familiar with now.

Housing growth declined in the US during the depression (1929 to the late 1930's) which was then followed by four years of war when again little housing was constructed as the war effort consumed all available resources. After the war, young couples with high birth rates had easy access to much needed low interest loans which drove an almost insatiable demand for low cost housing. William Levitt, a builder, along with his father Abraham and brother Alfred, purchased inexpensive land outside of town limits (the suburbs were invented) and from 1947 built highly planned communities of up to 17,000 new homes in New York, New Jersey and Pennsylvania. William had learnt mass production strategies building military housing for the navy during the war.

The homes in his Levittown communities were built of precut but not preassembled components on concrete slabs instead of foundations with basements by teams that had one of twenty-six specialised task. Levitt's homes could be produced in under six weeks and though inexpensive (initially $7990 which was three times the average annual wage) were well built and incorporated all mod cons including a TV and hi-fi. The down payment could be as little as one dollar and there was little risk to the builder as the mortgages were government guaranteed. At one stage he was finishing a house every sixteen minutes.

Levitt denied he was a builder but claimed instead to be a manufacturer. The efficiency of Levitt's construction methods quickly led to it becoming the industry standard in the US and later Australia. With the transformation of house construction from a cottage industry to a major manufacturing process the scene was set for a revolution in prefabricated trusses and frames.

Next month John Calvin Jureit

They Are Not Using Shipping Containers Are They?

Shipping containers being used to build a motel in Gatton

The motel next to our home is progressing and the earthworks which are of monumental proportions are almost completed but I was not impressed when a number of old shipping containers were delivered to site. Everybody was saying, "They are just storing material in them." But I could see that they had windows and wet areas inside. Anyway, a wise man once told me never to judge a half finished job so I held my peace. You can see from the first image above that they start looking pretty average (and that is being gracious) but, by the time they are completed, the units will not look too different to a normal building.

The shipping container houses the entry door and a very well appointed kitchen and bathroom, all built in China. On to that there is built a dry area using a concrete slab and timber frame. A conventional roof is then pitched over both areas. The builder, Jason Coulta of Coulta Crosby Design and Construction said the dry area used to be a container also in earlier projects but it proved less expensive to build on site. Jason said that this method of building reduced the construction cost by about $30%.

September 2016

More on Galvanised or Stainless Fasteners
Difference Between Hardwood, Pine and Cypress
Plastic Decking with Termites
Brief Trip to the Philippines
The Two Henry Fords of Housing

Difference Between Hardwood, Pine and Cypress

Recently I was asked to explain why a specification for a timber bollard has to be different depending on whether it was from hardwood, pine or cypress. I prepared the table below which clarified for him for guidance. For detailed specifications contact the author

Timber	Sapwood	Truewood	Heart/pith
Hardwood	Not durable – can be treated	Sometimes durable – cannot be treated	Unstable – cannot be treated
Cypress	Not durable – cannot be treated	Durable – cannot be treated	Structural – durable cannot be treated
Pine	Not durable – can be treated	Not durable – cannot be treated	Structural – not durable cannot be treated

Plastic Decking with Termites

One of my readers sent me these images of a well known brand of plastic timber composite decking. The deck had failed for the second time and was being replaced with timber. Most of us would not go back for a second helping. The builder noted when the decking split it swelled and locked in water which eventually attracted termites, note on the photos the splits in the sides of the decks which are cupped, split etc.

I am amazed how all reason goes out the window when choosing this type of product. It must stand the same rigorous scrutiny that a hardwood deck must pass. Contact me for the university testing I have had done. It will shock you. I am disappointed when people do not detail timber decks well and enforce good supply and construction details and then complain when when timber does not perform.

I know of a footbridge where plastic decking was used and then someone rode a horse on it. The poor animal fell straight through the decking. If it is a commercial application the decking must be able to withstand a commercial load with a minimal commercial deflection. It's all in my books

Brief trip to the Philippines

As I drove around Baguio, a resort city high in the hills of Luzon, I was surprised at how much concrete "timber" there was. When you have sent all your best logs to Japan and the US what else can you do but make concrete look like timber. This land, once renowned for its rainforests, now has a logging moratorium and only lesser species are being cut. My Australian readers should be very thankful for the good stewardship we have here.

As I love to talk, I gave two CPD sessions, one in Baguio on Architectural Timber Battens and in Manila on Building for Resilience - an Australian perspective. I met a bright young architect in Baguio that did his masters in Sydney and who is trying to reintroduce timber to that city. Baguio was very badly damaged in 1990 by an earthquake and the only buildings that withstood it were the timber ones.

The second speaking engagement was at a seminar in Manila run by the Emergency Architects division of the United Architects of the Philippines. The subject was building for resilience and the topic was Materials and Construction Technologies Through Timber. Special thanks to Michael Rayner for his assistance. There were very informative presentations on coco lumber bamboo and panels that used the strength of the loo roll (not the musician) centers. Habitat for Humanity a worthy organisation also gave very interesting reports. The picture on the left above is one of twelve homes built after Cyclone Yolanda by my host Pastor Galzote from coco lumber for $450 AUD each. A blessing for families that had lost absolutely everything. Have you booked a CPD session yet?

The Two Henry Fords of Housing Part 2 of 2

Researching my new book on timber joints I came across two men, William Levitt and John Calvin Jureit who would both be likened to Henry Ford in the way they transformed housing from being crafted one at a time into an assembly line construction that we are familiar with now. Last month I wrote about William Levitt.

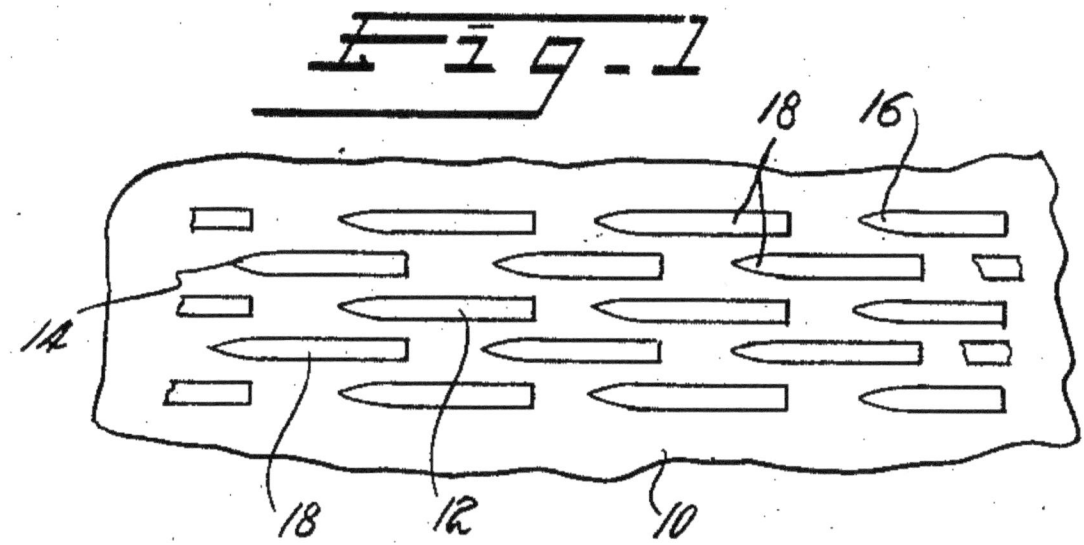

John Wesley Jureit, the other "Henry Ford" was another man influenced by World War 2 prefabrication in the Pacific. In 1949 he took on the first of two roles as the chief engineer in laboratories that tested building materials including trusses. In the first role, which was in a commercial laboratory, Jureit found he spent most of his time advising clients on how to improve their trusses rather than testing them. Despite the limitations of pre-nailplated trusses he could see that that "builders were already warming up to the fact that trusses were the way to go. I could already see it was going to be a big industry. We just needed a better way to do it". The "better way" came to him in a reflective moment in a church service after he had gone into private practice in 1955. His idea which revolutionised the construction industry was the first nailplate that did not require supplementary nailing. The name "Gang-Nail" came soon after. This nailplate shown in above had single straight teeth pressed from the plate which were long enough to secure the plate to the timber.

Many sawmills wanted to value add to their own wood but needed to set up at low cost though starting a truss plant in the beginning was not easy. The equipment needed to install plates simply did not exist or if they did exist the delivery times and cost precluded their use. Jureit became not just a plate manufacturer but also built the equipment to use them. He initially used a concrete vertical hydraulic press and steel table precision jigs to install them. The business was based on the razor blade principal – "give 'em the razors and they'll come back to you for blades"

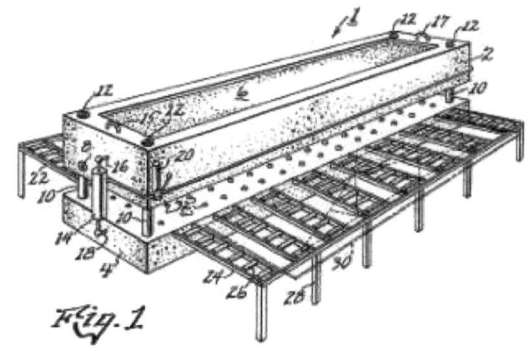

Edgar Stubbersfield

October 2016

Coconut Wood
New Guide for Mid Rise Developments
Lui the Wood Turner is a Fan of Tanacoat
Full Day Timber Seminar
Trusses - A Brief History

Coconut Wood

Last month I spoke about the logging moratorium in the Philippines, a land once heavily forested. What has taken the place of these hardwoods in the marketplace is cocowood. The image above is from a cocowood wholesaler outside of Manilla. The timber wholesales at 15 pesos per super foot ($A200 per m3) and retails at about 22-25 pesos per super foot ($A290 -330 per m3). There is only one length, 12 ft (3.6 m). Most is cut with a chainsaw and some with a Lucas style portable mill. If you dried this wood and run this material through a planer, it would look a very classy product. As this material is already entering the Australian market the question arises, "is it any good?". Simple question with a not so simple answer.

Strictly, coconut palm "wood" cannot be classified as wood. Cocowood is a blend of two different fibres: put simplistically, it is more like parallel cables embedded in foam. The outside is covered with a cortex that acts like bark. Coconut palms have neither heartwood nor annual growth rings and lack branches and therefore contain no knots in processed material.

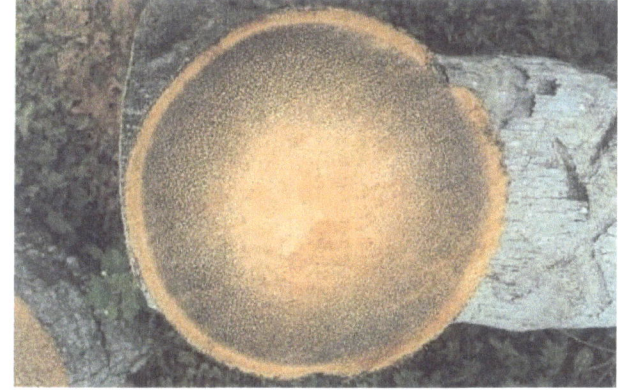

It is estimated that there are 120,000 hectares of over mature coconut plantations in the Asia-Pacific region that no longer produce enough coconuts to be profitable. The livelihood of millions of farmers are affected. The palms themselves are typically 25 metres high with a breast height diameter of between 25 and 35 cm. If these palms can be economically converted into sawn timber or veneer it provides a financial incentive for the farmers to remove these low productivity trees and replace them with either new coconut trees or other agricultural alternatives.

The outer portion of the palm is very dense (often between 800 to 1,170 kg/m3) with properties similar to many hardwoods. Unfortunately the inner section transitions between 400 to 600 kg/m3 in the intermediate zone down to 100-400 kg/m3 in the core. From the image above it is easy to identify the material with the highest property. High density cocowood can be used for flooring, furniture, joinery, panelling, pallets, plywood and veneers, utility poles (preservative-treated) and feature posts. Lower density material can be used for turnery, insulation, handicrafts and charcoal, firewood and a potting substrate for plants.

The Queensland Department of of Agriculture and Fisheries have published a number of excellent guides to cocowood and cocoveneer and are worth reading. Refer www.cocowood.net.

Only dinosaurs like me know what a super foot is. It is a volume of 12 inch x 12 inch by 1 inch and is how timber used to be sold in Australia. It is not as bad as a hoppus cubic foot which I also used to use also.

New WoodSolutions Design Guide for Mid-rise Developments

On May 1st 2016, The National Construction Code (NCC) was changed to allow the use of timber construction systems under the Deemed-to-Satisfy (DTS) Provisions for Class 2, 3 and 5 buildings up to 25 metres in effective height, known as 'mid-rise construction'. A new technical guide on the Wood Solutions website has been Created To help industry professionals realise the full benefits of the recent changes The new technical design guide, "Mid-rise Timber Buildings – Class 2, 3, and 5 Buildings" explains how to achieve the targeted fire and sound Performance Requirements. It is available for free download at http://bit.ly/MidRiseTimber.

Lui the Wood Turner is a Fan of Tanacoat

(Not a paid commercial)

Over the years I have made good friendships with people I have never met. Not Facebook friends but customers I only have had contact with by phone or email. One of these is Lui Greco of Lui's Wood Turning. Over the years Lui has been ringing me for advice and to purchase Tanacoat but was one of these people I had never met. Recently I decided to rectify that and directly above is a picture of Lui with one of his copy lathes. When I had to have some turned bollards made (top two images) I naturally turned to him (no pun intended) to make my square pieces round. I organised the copper caps and fitted them and the result is amazing I think. If you need wood turning Lui is a good man to know - see link below.

Lui particularly wanted to show me the timber awning over his entrance. It is five years old 20x20 spotted gum and gets a coat of Tanacoat every 9 months and it is in excellent shape. Incidentally that is tanacoat on the bollards also. Have you discovered Tanacoat yet? It was made by Arch, the timber treatment experts initially for Outdoor Structures Australia and that understanding of the properties of timber makes all the difference.

Turned posts look far better than natural rounds. This shelter used posts that were almost 4 metres long, 300 mm (finished starting at roughly 350mm) in diameter and tapered. They are too big for Lui's equipment (max 4.2 and starting at 300mm) but we were able to have them made locally here in Gatton on a large metal lathe. Hardwood turns beautifully and in my opinion is underutilised as a landscaping element..

Full Day Timber Seminar at Broncos League Club

On the 6th of October, Timber Queensland held a full day induction workshop entitled *Designing, specifying and building timber structures*. Colin Mckenzie, a legend in the timber industry, took one session and I delivered the other five. From the feedback it went well and Timber Queensland is considering holding more of these in the future.

If you are part of a council, government department or large professional office you should seriously consider holding one of these seminars in house. Contact Clarissa Brant, Communications Manager at Timber Queensland to organise a date. Her phone number is 07 3358 7906 and her email is clarissa@timberqueensland.com.au.

Trusses - A Brief History

(Extract from my upcoming book on timber joints)

Trusses have been with us since antiquity, possibly as early as the sixth century B.C. but certainly by the third century B.C. The tie beam truss is just a simple triangle with the rafters in compression and the tie beam in tension making a coherent system. This may well have originated in the Greek shrines in Sicily where the builders used larger unsupported spans than those used on the Greek mainland. While there is little evidence that the Greeks capitalised on the trusses ability to deliver large open spaces, the Romans certainly did utilise them. They were able to span over 30 metres by the time of Augustus. Unfortunately we no longer have evidence available about how these joints were constructed. One researcher commented "There is no question, however, that the timber truss was extremely strong and for this reason is still a fundamental component of modern timber framing." For all their innovation, there is little or no evidence of any engineering theory being employed and, as floor frames were generally heavier than needed, the same is likely to have applied to the trusses.

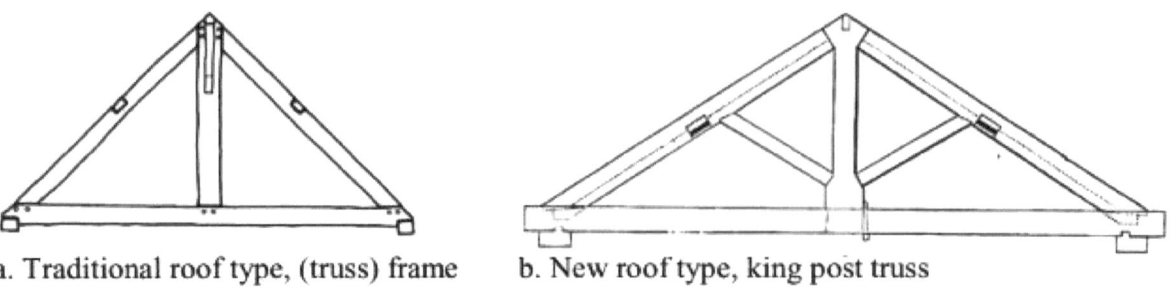

a. Traditional roof type, (truss) frame   b. New roof type, king post truss

Transition of king post truss.

In these early trusses, the ceiling beam had to carry the full load of the roof with their own bearing capacity. Some scholars think that the tie beam (bottom cord) in some of these trusses from antiquity could have been as deep as 500 mm! While these timbers may well have been available in a world that still had large almost virgin forests, it was not sustainable. We see over the intervening years the timber sizes decreasing and now modern builders who wish to take advantage of a truss's obvious strength must do so with much smaller sizes and improved truss designs and connections. This improvement was started with the development of the king post truss. Initially in ancient Greece this was a compression member where the post was attached to the ceiling beam and supported the weight of the rafters, being fitted under or into them where they met at the apex. In this arrangement the load on the ceiling beam was increased. But the king post design transitioned whereby the post extended to the top of the apex and the rafters fitted into the post, in effect hanging the post from the rafters which could then be used to support what is now a tie beam. Members that were subject to bending were now primarily axially loaded which transferred much greater loads into the base of the rafter where it joined the ceiling beam. This loading allowed for smaller sizes which are needed for larger spans. To this in time were added different diagonal and post arrangements but the approach to the design of trusses was still empirical.

Palladio's 36 m bridge over the Cismon River. Trajan's 33 m span trusses over the Danube (from Trajan's column).

The start of the transition from empirical design to a scientific approach is often attributed to Andrea Palladio and his widely disseminated 1570 treatise *i quattro libri dell'Architettura* where he describes a number of timber bridges without intermediate supports. Palladio claims them as "inventions" as he believed them to be different to anything seen previously. His book contains the oldest detailed designs for bridge trusses including that of the Cismon river which spanned 36 metres. The Romans were able to achieve bridge spans of 33 metres but these were not simply supported structures but gained the benefit of continuity from the adjacent truss (refer Trajan's bridge above). The joints he designed would not be improved upon for at least 200 years but their very labour intensive nature highlight the difficulty of making effective connections for large span trusses. Another contribution was the development of modularity with standard sized members (for Cismon bridge 360 mm high and 270 mm wide) and components that could be prefabricated and quickly assembled.

Trajan's bridge was essentially an arch built of timber instead of stone and at the beginning of the 19th century "arch structures were considered the most suitable structural system for large span [timber] bridges". In the arch there were, in effect, no joints compared to the multiplicity of joints and greater deflection in the truss. But the rapid expansion of railways in North America bought a new approach. The profit driven and highly competitive environment forced builders to seek solutions that required a minimum amount of time and effort to achieve the desired outcome. Wood and labour were relatively inexpensive and steel was expensive so these solutions were frequently wooden. This would lead to a rush of new truss types, many bearing the names of their inventors. Some of these are:

- Burr arch truss (Thomas Burr, patented 1817)
- Town truss (Ithiel Town, patented 1820)
- Howe truss (William Howe, patented 1840)
- Bowstring arch truss (Squire Whipple, patented 1841)
- Pratt truss (Thomas and Caleb Pratt, invented 1844)
- Warren truss (James Warren, patented 1848).

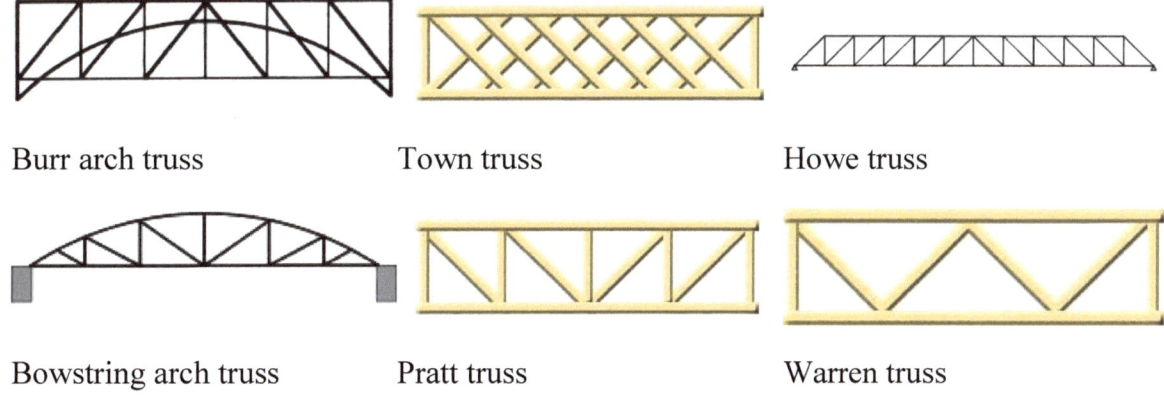

Illustrations of different truss types.

It should be noted that these trusses predate the first scientific publications on the theory of trusses which were not released until 1851 and then were in German.

(Note - images of truss types are taken from wikipedia. Refer to https://en.wikipedia.org/wiki/Truss_bridge#Warren_truss for credits on images)

November 2016

Choosing the Correct Decking Fastener - Guest author
Free Book - Covered Bridges and the Birth of American Engineering
Width to Thickness Ratio - An Old Bridge Revisited
Corroding Galvanised Joist Hanger - New Guidelines
Three New Wood Solutions Technical Guides
Guest Speaker at Brandon and Associates Symposium

The following insightful article was contributed by guest author, Herb Kuhn, Managing Director Simpson Strong-Tie Australia. Over recent months I have had a lot to say about corroding fasteners but Herb's addition to the debate is that you must also consider 'ductility'. Herb has been very helpful as I put my next book together, *Timber Joints*, actually many people from across the industry and academia have been very helpful.

Choosing The Correct Decking Fasteners
Part 1 of 2

As we continue to spend more time in the outdoors and more houses have the "extra outdoor room" we expect the decking that we lay to last and perform the same as our internal floors. There are many decisions to be made that can affect the long term performance and look of decking. The use of screws to fasten down decking has become more popular due to the fact that timber decking moves with heat and cold, moisture and dry. Nails will allow the decking to move as it does and typically nails allow them to do this as they are carbon steel. This constant movement can, over time, mean that the nail wriggles out of the joist and that may leave the head of the nail exposed. You can hammer it down again, however more movement will see the nail heads come up again.

Screws will have a better hold in the joist and this will restrict the timber movement, however screws are case hardened. This hardening process makes the screw tougher, however bending from side to side can cause work hardening and possibly breakage. Hardwood timber is a living growing thing and the movement caused by moisture and temperature means that if we prefer to use screws because they hold better, then we need to look for fasteners that move with it, or are ductile. We agree that hardened carbon steel is not very ductile so we now recommend stainless steel for all hardwood decking applications. It is an alloy and the make up of the stainless screw is that it can be bent in different directions without breaking and this is a better long term fastener for exposed decking that needs to deal with the elements.

Corrosion performance is definitely one consideration and proximity to swimming pools and the ocean should automatically direct us to use stainless steel as opposed to plated steel screws. However ductility should be of equal consideration if we are looking for a long lasting deck structure. A hardwood deck that is fully exposed to the rain and direct sun will expand with the rain and shrink with the dry, it will dry out without humidity and swell with it and all of this creates movement of the decking boards. Keeping the decking well oiled will reduce the affect that these conditions have on the timber, however the use of stainless steel screws has a significant benefit in ensuring that the fastener does not break with the movement of the decking.

Thank you Herb. There is more from Herb next month when he gives good advice about ductility of screws used with steel joists. While this is not a paid advertisement, it is worth looking at the connectors that Simpson Strong-Tie have available. Their range is at least double that of most connector suppliers.

Covered Bridges and the Birth of American Engineering

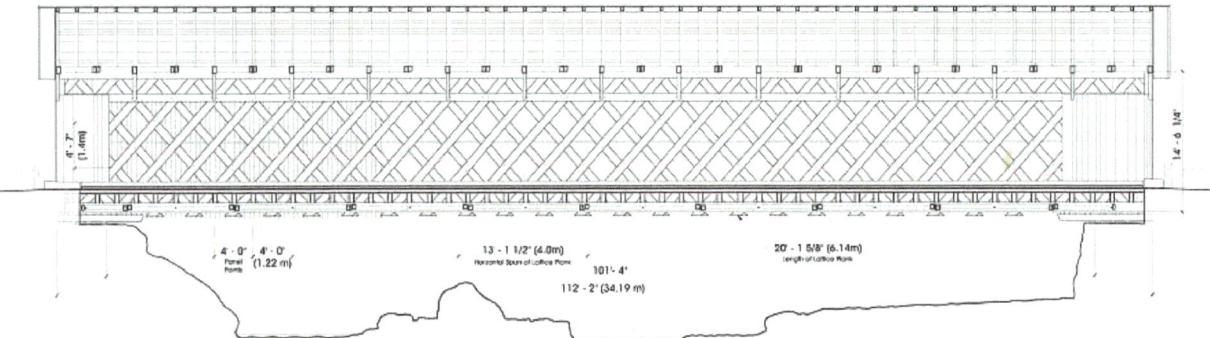

A fascinating and fortunately free publication about covered bridges has been released by the National Parks Service in the US. This book examines the development of wood trusses and covered bridge construction, profiles the pioneering craftsmen and engineers involved, explores the function of trusses in covered bridges, and looks at the preservation and future of these distinctly American bridges. The editors have collaborated with some of the leading historians and engineers of historic covered bridges in the country to produce this volume.

Download the medium resolution book at https://www.nps.gov/hdp/CoveredBridges2015med.pdf

Download the high resolution book at https://www.nps.gov/hdp/CoveredBridges2015.pdf

For some reason I cannot explain, Australia has obstinately refused to cover its timber bridges despite the compelling case to do so.

Here is an image of the only covered bridge I know of in Australia. We were heavily involved with this job which is situated in Sandgate, Queensland.

Width to Thickness Ratio - An Old Bridge Revisited

Some years ago I sold the log footbridge illustrated above to the Brisbane City Council. At the time we discussed the width to thickness ratio of the decking. One authority said the ratio was not to exceed 3 to 1 e.g. 105x35 mm. I looked them in the eye and said I was not having trouble with 145x35 which is 4.14 to 1 which was then completely true. I was milling the timber sourced from the Lockyer Valley in our own mill and was not having issues. Later we closed the mill and started sourcing timber billets from a wide variety of locations in Queensland and then the trouble started. I had two claims against 145x35 so I dropped it from the range and now recommend a ratio of 3.5 to 1.

I had always wondered if I had misled my clients so, when I had the opportunity to check it out after many years I was a little worried that the deck might have been cupped. The deck was perfectly straight without a hint of cupping. None of us now have the ability to control where timber is sourced from to such a fine degree so my recommendation is still 3.5 to 1. That means that 120x35 and 145x45 are in and 145x35 and 195x45 are out.

Corroding Galvanised Joist Hanger - New Guidelines

The corroding galvanised joist hanger in a timber deck was photographed at the student village at the University of Southern Queensland. It is not particularly old and not a high hazard area. It illustrates the wisdom behind Timber Queensland and the different nail plate manufacturers agreed position in 2016 on where to use stainless and where to use galvanised connectors. You can read this in Timber Queensland's *Technical Data Sheet 35, Corrosion Resistance of Metal Connectors*. This guide identifies different corrosion zones:

- Sea spray zone (less than 1 km from a surf coast, 100 m from bayside areas)
- Coastal zone (1 – 10 km from surf coast, or 1 km from bayside)
- Industrial zone (close to complexes emitting corrosive gasses)
- Special Hazard (e.g. enclosed swimming pools where stainless may even corrode and beyond the scope of the data sheet)
- Low hazard zone (anywhere outside the four areas listed above)

This is then broken down into 3 exposure conditions

- Enclosed (within a closed roof, floor and wall cavity)
- Sheltered (subject to wind-blown salt but not washed with rain, e.g. open garages and sub-floors)

- Exposed (experiencing both weather and rain, e.g. decks and pergolas).

In all exposed allocations in the four areas covered by the guide, 316 grade stainless is required (or else specially prepared plates) meaning the above joist hanger should have been stainless. For the sheltered applications, an area not differentiated by some recommendations prior to 2016, a standard Z275 (275 grammes of galvanising per m2) can only be used in the Low Hazard Zone, other applications require either stainless (Seaspray Zone) or the addition of soft seal paint (Coastal and Industrial). Where there is little risk of corrosion such as in an enclosed and **sealed** roof area Z275 can be used even in a Seaspray Zone. Further, these recommendations are for *non treated* timber and those treated with waterborne preservatives can require additional paint protection on top of heavier galvanising which, for simplicity, basically forces you to stainless.

If you do not have the latest recommendations avail yourself of them from your plate supplier or read Timber Queensland Technical Data Sheet #35 'Corrosion Resistance of Metal connectors' for complete details.

Three New Wood Solutions Technical Guides

Wood Solutions are continuing the roll out of very high quality technical guides in the EXPAN series with another three having been just released. The EXPAN guides are based on the results of years of research by the Structural Timber Innovation Company (STIC), a unique collaboration between Australian and New Zealand commercial and academic partners to create innovative structural timber solutions. The EXPAN Technical Design Guides are available for free download from WoodSolutions.com.au.

Timber Rivet Connection: The aim of the Design Guide #34 is to provide an aid for engineers for designing timber rivet connections in structural seasoned wood products including seasoned sawn timber, glulam and laminated veneer lumber (LVL).

Floor Diaphragms in Timber Buildings: The first part of the Design Guide #35 presents the terminology, concept and design of timber diaphragms with their connections to the lateral load-resisting system (LLRS). The second part reviews a design example of a timber–concrete diaphragm and its connections to the LLRS. The diaphragm is subjected to the wind load applied perpendicular to its long side.

Engineered Wood and Fabrication Specification: The last Design Guide from this series, #36, provides a summary of fabrication and installation specifications of engineered wood products, i.e. laminated veneer lumber (LVL) and glulam. It provides recommendations for different steps of the timber structure supply chain, including storage, handling and transportation, erection and assembly. It includes insect and mould preventions and moisture design considerations.

Guest speaker at Brandon & Associates Symposium

On the 16th of this month I was a guest speaker at the annual symposium held by Brandon and Associates held in Chinchilla, Queensland. Brandons are Queensland's largest rural based consulting engineering firm, operating across South-West and Central Queensland. The positive feedback was that it filled the "gap between theory and practical". Apparently I scored 4.78 out of 5 and was the rated the best speaker over the two days. Call me if you would like your own Ted Talk - CPD points can be earned.

December 2016

Choosing the Correct Decking Fastener - Guest author
Tube Nuts - An Old Bridge Revisited
Largest Timber Gable Truss in Australia

Last month I ran *Part One* on the importance of understanding ductility when considering decking fasteners with a very good article by Herb Kuhn, Managing Director of Simpson Strong-Tie Australia. Herb has more to say this month but before we hear from him, I will provide some extra background to the problem below.

Choosing the Correct Decking Fasteners
Part 2 of 2 - Screws with steel decking

Steel joist used on verandah badly corroding. Broken screws in C section steel joists
Image courtesy Contrast Constructions.

Blackbutt with high acidity (pH 3.6) used on steel joists - not something I would advise. (The image of the broken screw above is from this deck.)

When we were writing our LifePlus Decking Guide (only $22.00 a real bargain), we wanted to include information about how to attach our 88x21 decking to steel joists. It is not as easy as it seems as you can easily be swapping well known and easily "sortable" issues for ones that are not as well known and not as easy to sort. So we wrote to Lysaghts asking for how we detail to avoid the four issues we saw which were:-

- Increased acidity of new treatments
- Lipped profiles of C and Z sections holding moisture
- Decreased torsional stiffness
- Screw manufacturers not certifying their screws when going from timber to steel

These days I would now add a fifth issue - the acidity of the timber.

After a very long time (two years) we got a verbal reply that they did not approve of their steel joists being used with timber. Later a technical bulletin was issued CTB-13 *Contact with Timber* which basically says, if not CCA treated, they advise against its use. That would be the end of the matter except that a Lysaght publication *Construction of a Lysaght QuickaFloor* outlines how to make a verandah floor with their product and does not appear to mention that you are not to use timber decking. A phone call indicated that decking would have to be screwed or nailed with a hardened twisted shank nail as with the internal floor sheeting instructions. A publication I found more helpful was the *Duragal Flooring System* published by Onesteel. Their guide gives design solutions for all the issues I sought guidance on, which includes the use of a joist sealing tape between the decking and the joist. From here it gets complicated...

The Duragal guide prohibits the use of solvent based decking oils (page 9) as that may damage the sealing tape - and, in our opinion, the best domestic decking oil, Tanacoat, is solvent based and your decking should be oiled all around and then done thereafter as needed - with Tanacoat of course! (Tanacoat is now low in aromatics which is generally what attacks the strip so it should be fine but your builder may substitute the good oil for something of lower cost which may cause issues). Norton Flashtac which is specified for sealing the ends of the joist could be used over the whole joist and it won't be attacked by the solvents in cheap decking oils but, last time I priced Flashtac, it was $4.00 per metre so it is not going to happen due to its cost. The Duragal guide then advises against using decking screws to fasten the decking to the joist but recommends hardened nails. However in my opinion people are going to continue to use screws. Over to you Herb (not a paid advertisement).

"In our experience areas like North East Victoria and the High Country are the most extreme and as you get further from the coast the humidity variation is most extreme. West of the Great Divide is the other area that is a real challenge for us, again due to the hot and dry summer and then if there is large amounts of rain in the winter or wet seasons, this creates the challenging environment that we need to deal with.

It is also worth mentioning that when fixing Hardwood decking to steel joists, in bushfire prone areas, that Bi-Metal screws are the ONLY solution, again due to the ductility of stainless steel. Bi-metal screws have a carbon steel drill point, wings and the first 4 threads and the remainder of the fastener is 316 stainless for optimum ductility." Herb added later that his screws have a zinc coating to minimise the potential for corrosion due to dissimilar metals. Image courtesy of Simpson Strong-Tie

Tube Nuts - An Old Bridge Revisited

Last Month I commented on an old bridge I supplied the Brisbane City Council and the lessons it showed about the importance of correct width to thickness ratio.

The bridge makes extensive use of tube nuts we call Man-O-War nuts. They are M12, have a mushroom head with a Hex drive and are made from stainless steel. The tube measured 30mm long and is 16 mm on the outside. But why add the extra cost when a nut would have sufficed?

When I first started manufacturing timber landscaping such as barbecue tables I learnt of a case where a young child severely disfigured her face on a protruding bolt when she fell against it - similar to the one illustrated. The personal pain and anguish for the child and the family and on the supplier, even if he was a heartless so and so, would have felt the pain of the litigation that followed. I thought, "It is not worth going down that path for the few dollars saved". We made it a policy to use tube nuts where we had to use bolts and try as much as possible to use coachscrews and batten screws.

They also look a lot neater than countersunk bolts. Compare the two bollards above, one by us on the left and the other by the lower priced supplier. Undoubtedly ours looks better. Do you want to know how to achieve this finish? Look at the December 2015 Newsletter which explains how. Man-O-War nuts can be purchased from Outdoor Structures Australia. Call Tammy on 0403 601 041

Largest Timber Gable Truss in Australia

A 39.6m hardwood truss using shearplates under construction at Tocumwal, NSW during World War 2. Image Courtesy Associate Professor Gregory Nolan

Truss made with shearplate connectors at Werribee aerodrome. Image courtesy of Owen Peake

An example of the use of shear plate construction is the heritage listed Werribee aerodrome hangars constructed during World War Two. These are an American design, re-engineered from pine to Australian Hardwood with clear spans reaching 130 ft (39.6 m) Like the Igloo, timber framing was again used as steel was in short supply. One author wrote, "Architecturally these structures are unique as they are the first long span trusses recorded that use timber as tension web members. They [were in 1996 and still believed to be so] the longest clear span gable shaped timber truss buildings known in Australia." Similar trusses were built elsewhere including Tocumwal.

The 96 ft (29.3 m) hangar used a double 8x3 inch (200x75 mm) for the top cord a double 6x3 inch (150x75 mm) for the bottom cord. The main diagonals reduced from double 6x3 inch (150x75 mm) at the centre to 4x3 inch (100x75 mm) and ancillary bracing is single 4x2 inch (100x50 mm). These trusses were, in a sense, experimental as up till then timber in major projects had been seasoned but there was no longer time for this. Unseasoned timber had to be used and the engineers had to learn how to overcome the difficulties that caused.

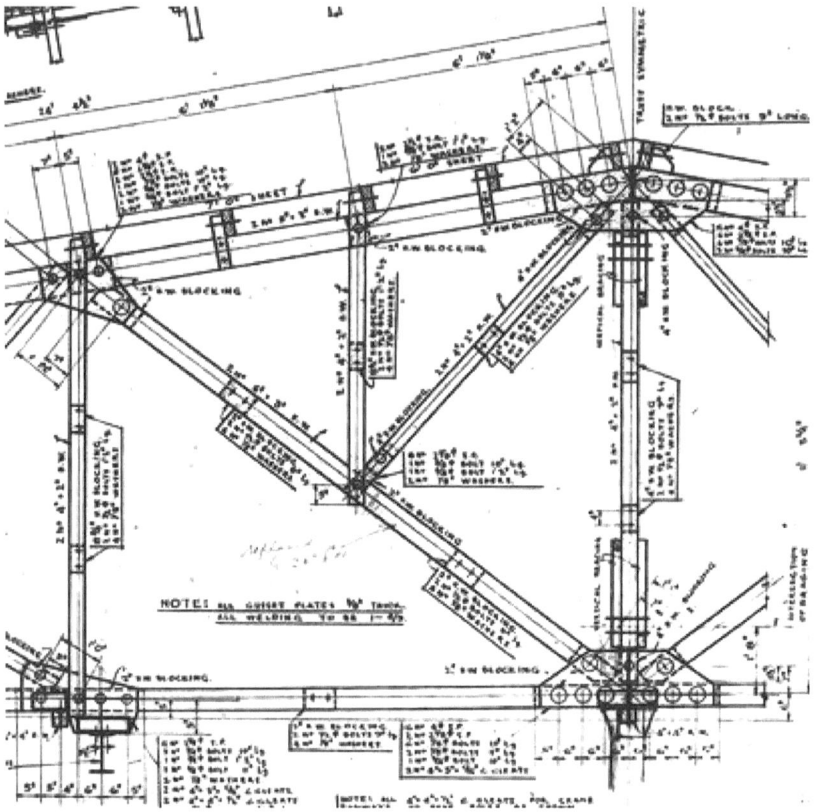

Detail of truss in 29.3 m Werribee Hangar. Drawing courtesy of Owen Peake.

While no problems were reported with the shorter 96 ft spans, the 130 ft truss initially had considerable problems. The 130ft (39.6 m) span trusses were constructed with a straight-line camber of 8 inches (200 mm) at the centre of the span but when measured 9 months after construction, deflections from the cambered position ranged from 184 mm to 238 mm. Deflection, roughly the quarter points of the span were the lowest, giving a double festooned appearance. This required the trusses to be propped and re-cambered. Gregory Nolan speculated that, "It is probable that the stresses allowed were just too great for satisfactory performance with green hardwood." With the seasoning of the timber no further problems were reported and those of both length that were inspected in 1992 were performing satisfactorily.

2017

January 2017

A Dreadful Deck in Canberra is Finally Made Safe
Choosing the Correct Decking Fasteners
Natural Images E Newsletter

A Dreadful Deck in Canberra is Finally Made Safe

From the air, the deck in Queen Elizabeth Drive in Canberra looks stunning, but as our political masters keep telling us, "The devil is in the detail"! Back in 2005 I was asked to quote for the material but even a casual glance and some primary school arithmetic told me that it would not work. The timber specification, to my recollection, was 200x50 F17 spotted gum laid with a 5 mm gap. If you cramp your boards to remove any spring you have a target gap of 17 mm which is dangerous and way outside the disability code requirements. (the mathematics are 200 mm x 6% shrinkage = 12 mm then add the laying gap of 5 mm). So I wrote to one of the professionals involved offering to help them make it a success but sadly it was rebuffed.

The inevitable happened. One of my readers was doing the circuit on his bike and the front wheel dropped down between the gaps and was injured as he went headfirst over the handlebars. The deck was then blocked off to bikes and should have been totally blocked off as it was dangerous. Of course, timber will have received the blame, not the design.

I visited Canberra again last Christmas and saw that the deck had finally been taken up and re-laid with spacers inserted to take up the gaps.

As for the specification, much of the decking did not meet any F rating and, from what I could see, only lip service was paid to supplying to the nominated grade. You would expect that the contractor obtained three prices and took the lowest price. Those suppliers that quoted to supply to grade did not get a look in. There is no point nominating an F grade if you don't know what it actually looks like or if you are not going to enforce it. And decking has requirements that goes far beyond F grades!! Projects like this should require independent confirmation of grade, and not just to grade but to a suitable grade!! My book *Grading Hardwood* is a must if you are going to specify decking for a major project.

Back then, I would have assisted at no charge just to get my Deckwood specified now I charge to review plans but, as this project shows, it is money well spent.

The heart centre 300x300 seats were far from a success. Next month I will deal with how to make them perform as you expect. Again, it is just attention to detail.

Choosing the Correct Decking Fasteners
Part 3 of 2 - Nails

Two months ago I ran *Part One* on decking fasteners where guest author, Herb Kuhn, Managing Director of Simpson Strong-Tie Australia. spoke about the importance of understanding ductility when considering decking fasteners. Herb had more to say in december about decking screws to steel so there was *Part Two*. I realised that whatever I said about using screws people will ignore it and still nail so here is some food for thought and that is why it is *Part Three* of two!

I designed a weather exposed ramp for a friend using LifePlus which was to be screwed to the joists. The builder was told to screw the decking, "Yes, Yes" and then when he found it was more expensive than nailing simply nailed the decking instead. So much so for a specification but he at least did hand nail it using a 50 mm domed head nail. While these nails work satisfactorily under a roof they are eventually forced out if they are weather exposed. Dome head also have the disadvantage of preventing the deck being sanded at a later date.

	Hand Nail						Machine Nail											Screw
Shank	Plain	Screw	Ring	Plain	Plain	Plain	Plain	Screw	Screw	Screw	Screw	Screw	Ring	Ring	Ring	Screw	Screw	Counter
Head type	Bullet	Dome	Flat	Bullet	Bullet	Bullet	Flat	Dome	Dome	Dome	Dome	Dome	Dome	Dome	Dome	Dome	Dome	sunk
Nail material	HD-Gal	HD-Gal	HD-Gal	SS	HD-Gal	SS	HD-Gal	HD-Gal Ad	HD-Gal Ad	SS	SS	SS-Ad	HD-Gal Ad	SS-Ad	SS	HD-Gal	SS	SS
Size	50 x 2.8	50 x 2.8	50 x 2.8	50 x 2.8	65 x 2.8	65 x 2.8	50 x 2.5	50 x 2.5	50 x 2.5	50 x 2.5	50 x 2.5	50 x 2.5	52 x 2.5	50 x 2.5	65 x 2.5	65 x 2.5	8g x 50
Timber Joist	Hw	Sw	Sw	Hw	Sw	Sw	Hw	Hw	Sw	Hw	Sw	Hw	Sw	Sw	Sw	Sw	Sw	Hw
Test	1	2	3	21	4	22	5	7	20	8	11	9	10	13	14	15	16	19
Shank dia (mm)	2.8	2.9	3.0	2.8	2.9	2.8	2.5	2.5	2.5	2.5	2.5	2.4	2.5	2.5	2.5	2.5	2.5	-
Thread dia (mm)	-	3.1	3.1	-	-	-	-	2.7	2.7	2.7	2.7	2.6	2.6	2.6	2.7	2.8	2.6	4.1
Length to head (mm)	48	48	49	48	63	63	43	50	50	49	49	51	50	50	48	63	64	47
Ave. withdrawal (kN)	2.6	1.9	1.6	1.8	1.1	1.0	2.0	3.0	1.2	3.3	1.6	2.0	1.6	1.8	1.7	1.6	0.9	10.8
Max (kN)	3.2	3.1	2.9	2.9	1.8	1.9	2.4	4.2	1.8	4.5	2.5	3.3	2.5	2.6	2.9	2.5	1.3	12.8
Min (kN)	1.8	1.0	0.7	0.7	0.5	0.4	1.2	1.8	0.7	2.4	1.1	1.0	0.5	1.1	0.7	0.7	0.6	8.2

Gun nails are another matter. The Forest and Wood Products Development Corporation funded a study into the effectiveness of different decking fasteners The results are frightening as the summary of the findings above show. Two galvanised bullet head nails into a hardwood joist had an average withdrawal of 2.6 kN. Gun nails could be down to 0.9 kN!!! I had a customer who absolutely insisted on gun nailing his deck. I found out the brand of the nail with the highest rating on this table and sold them to him. He did not thank me as the deck now creaks underfoot. Pneumatic nail guns may have added speed but at the expense of (according to many) quality. "A contractors selection of the appropriate fastening method remains a choice based not only on strength, but also on value and workmanship."[1]

Compare the hold down of the best nails to an 8# screw at 10.8 kN and then consider that you will use a 10# on hardwood.

---

[1] Sauter, David. *Landscape Construction, 3rd Edition.* (Delmar: Cenage Learning, 2011), 90.

Natural Images E Newsletter Released

My friend, Tony Neilson, a long standing identity in the timber industry publishing and conservation photo-journalist has just released a new E-Newsletter called *Natural Images*. It is intended for people with an interest in sustainability and the natural environment. The image above is from the first edition.

Birds – his favourite subject from nature – carry many of the site's messages: "For 100 million years they have been a great success story. Now, they are seriously threatened by the hand of man."

But there is much more to this site than bird images. So why not register now for the free monthly newsletter. The copy's good and the 'scenery' isn't too bad either.

February 2017

Using Heart in Timber
Case History - Salt Shed in the USA
Span Chart Software

Using Heart In Timber

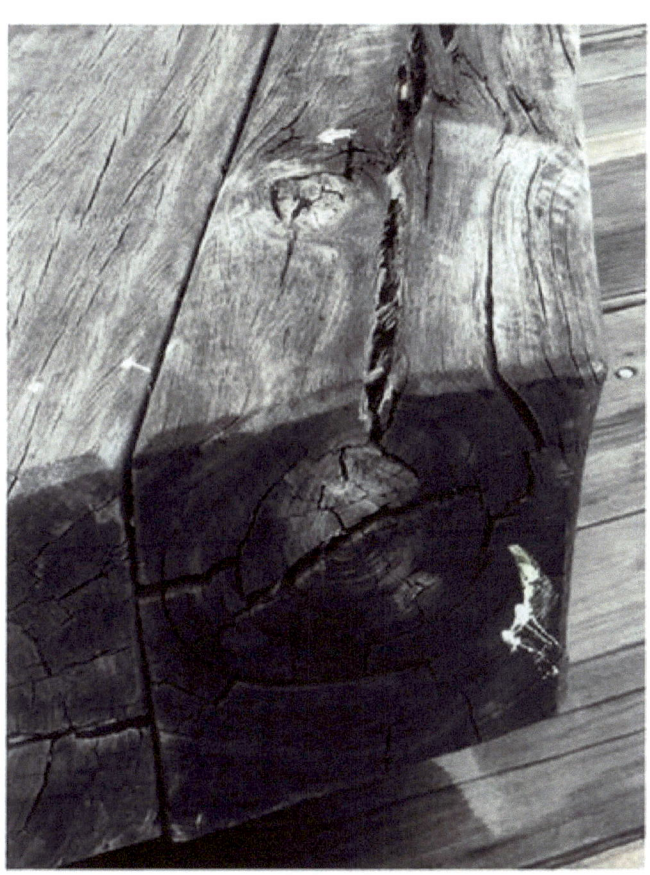

Last month I featured a dangerous deck in Canberra that had finally been made safe. There were a number of 300x300 mm heart in seats on the deck that were not a success either and could never be. They were not detailed in a way that accommodated the different properties of heart in timber to that which is heart free. Some of these seats are dangerous as poor detailing has allowed finger entrapments to develop. But heart in material is a great resource, you just have to work with its limitations. So how do you deal with this sort of material?

Firstly what is right with this design is that it is not bolted through the top allowing moisture into the heart. That can cause early degrade.

With these large sawn sizes, the outside is losing moisture and shrinking but the centre is retaining its moisture and so staying the same size. Something has to give so it tears down at least one of the faces. The seat on the right in the top image has the heart off centre and it has been placed with the shortest distance to the heart uppermost and that is where it is splitting. The same with the image to the right, splitting is to the surface closest to the heart. Good practice would see the heart placed closest to the underside. There is no obligation under AS 2082 to cut the material with the heart in the centre but it is none the less poor sawing. But good practice alone is not going to ensure there will be no or very minimal splitting.

This image to the right shows that despite the heart being in the centre of the three pieces, splitting still occurred. Ultimately the only way you will stop it splitting is by the use of expansion grooves. On a 200 mm you only need one but on a 300 mm you may need two. my technique was to make the groove 25 mm deep and 3 mm wide. For the tops it is wise to also arris the top of the groove and also for all sides if used as posts. The gaps open and close as needs be and any tear is below the saw cut. These expansion grooves need to be cut very soon after milling - say one week and an absolute maximum of two weeks after.

Another important consideration with any heart in material is to keep the minimum size to 175 mm e.g. 300x175 mm (as was required under AS 2082 - 2000) but better still 200 mm.

Three faces was enough to groove on a 200x200, one was not enough as the post opened up too much. The next four images show each side of a 12 year old (approx) 300x200 mm bollard outside my old office. On three sides the gap, after initially opening, has closed tight and one side has opened a little. These expansion joints really do work.

So if we had to write a specification for a box heart seat I would say:

- xyz mm X xyz mm, heart centre hardwood,
- acceptable species are spotted gum, tallowwood and ironbark
- cut with the heart in the centre, not significantly to one side.
- Cut an expansion joint/s into each face within one week of milling. The expansion joint/s will be 3 mm wide and 25 mm deep.
- arris the edge of the expansion joint on the top face.
- Where timber is supplied with the heart significantly to one side acceptance is subject to the (insert profession)'s approval for use and give instructions as to placement.

Remember the number of expansion joints will depend on the width and also remember that 300x300 is hard to find in suitable species).

Of course when it comes to 200x200 and you don't want to be disappointed, just purchase the product I developed called the Pioneer Post. One size only 192x192. Caps are not an option if being used as bollards. Wilson Timbers are still manufacturing some of my products. Contact Tammy on **T** (07) 3277 1988 I **F** (07) 3277 6435 I M 0403 601 041 **E** tammy@wilsontimbers.com

Salt Storage Shed East Windsor, New Jersey, United States
(Not a paid advertisement)

When I was writing about split rings and shearplates in my latest book, *Timber Joints,* I came to appreciate how good they were in distributing loads in timber connections. Unfortunately I could not see that they were available in Australia any longer. Nate Erde-Wollheim of Portland Bolt in the US who supplies these connectors was incredibly helpful so I am happy to give them a mention by showing this unusual 2016 project in a corrosive environment. Note that timber does not rust!!

The State of New Jersey required additional capacity to store salt which is used to clear snow from roadways during wintery weather. A new salt storage shed was proposed in order to increase the lane miles that could be accommodated by existing facilities. This specific salt storage facility is responsible for housing approximately 5,400 tons of salt as well as maintenance vehicles which distribute the salt. The arches on this building stand over 14' (4.26 m) above the concrete walls and the building extends approximately 150' (45.7 m) in length.

Portland Bolt supplied nearly 2,200 bolts and over 500 shear plates on this project and all of the items were hot dipped galvanised to provide corrosion resistance on the fasteners.

If you are considering using shear plates or split rings the contact is Nate Erde-Wollheim. Email: nate@portlandbolt.com and the phone from Australia is : 0011 1 855 739 0833.

In Australia we have not built structures in timber that approach the spans that were achieved during World War 2. Here are some links to what our forefathers achieved with shear plates.

Span Chart Software

Timber Solutions is a design software package developed initially to generate tables for AS 1684 Residential Timber-framed Construction Standard. It is now available as a stand-alone package which complements the Standard. The software package can output generic tables or can be used to provide structural design solutions for individual houses. Outputs include timber sizes, tie-down loads and bracing loads as per AS 1684

March 2017

New Book on Timber Joints All but Complete
A Decent Garden Wall
How Long Will a Timber Deck Last?
Stump Caps
Case History - RothoBlass Headquarters – Italy

New Book On Timber Joints All But Complete

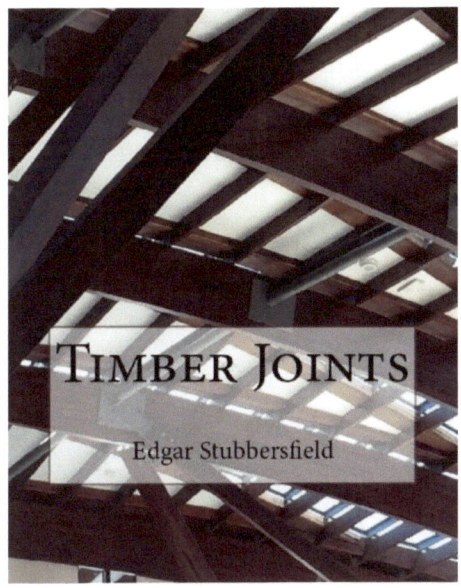

Apart from two images where the copyright is alluding me, my book on timber joints is complete. Despite those two images I am offering it for sale now particularly as it contains a very useful section which guides you in the selection of stainless or galvanised fasteners. Each chapter has all been checked by experts in the field. Price $50.

A friend wrote back after reading the relevant chapter and said "I have read, with interest, the extract from the book. The references to suppliers of special screws and wood rivets is useful.In particular, I have identified a screw by Rothoblaas suitable for the external metal gussets that I am designing to repair a 740 x115mm laminated beam portal frame in Brisbane."

A Decent Garden Wall

I recently had a phone call from another consultant looking for a picture of a decent garden wall to illustrate a guide he was writing on the subject. He was like me, having plenty of images of "dodgy" work but a dearth of success stories. I really had to think, but the answer was staring me in the face, my own garden wall. I followed the Timber Queensland guidelines for fences and garden walls and it worked. It is not rocket science.

My garden wall which also incorporates a fence was built c. 2000 and the sleepers, which predate 1992, were simply reused from an earlier wall. The posts are F17 ironbark, heart free, from Muckerts Sawmill in Laidley. They are 900 mm in the ground and are set in no fines concrete. There is no decay. The poor fencing contractor had never heard of no fines concrete or used timber of that quality (and he is probably the lowest tenderer for your next job). The rails are spotted gum (I think). I knew what I needed, I knew where to get it, I was not afraid to pay what it cost and I did not let the contractor purchase the material. All I would do differently now is use stainless steel fasteners. You are not likely to have that control for your garden wall. In last July's newsletter I suggested that you are probably better off with concrete.

Because it is also difficult to produce timber fencing of consistent quality, and it would look dreadful in concrete, I wrote the timber fencing guide to help you bring them in successfully, time after time It might even inspire you to deliver work like that by my friends at Kurata Co in Japan. Here is an image of gate they recently built in Japan using spotted gum.

How Long Will a Timber Deck Last?

Recently I was in Cairns doing CPD sessions for Ports North. After the session we went and had a look at their timber decks. Now you have to admit that portside in Cairns is about as hard an environment as you would expect to encounter. The deck shown above is about 14 years old and is in great shape and replacement is not on the horizon. I was told that they expected to achieve 30 years with an acceptable level of maintenance. But they give their deck love, treating it regularly but, very importantly, they love it with the right kind of love, they ensure there is no film buildup on the surface to trap moisture. Incidentally, I have commented on the handrail before. It ticks all the boxes for best practice in handrail design.

Here is a very different deck built in 1986 and photographed in 2012. From the day it was put in it had no love at all, but, being here in Gatton which seems to be in perpetual drought, they still only replaced the deck after 29 years.

So longevity is dependent on where the deck is and whether it has the right amount of love. The factors that I have found essential for a long deck life are:

- Use the most durable species and the highest grades. Specifications like F14/F17 lead to heartache (Deckwood takes the mystery out of it)
- Ensure the width the thickness ration does not exceed 3.5 to 1 (no 145x35)
- Use a rough sawn face
- Oil regularly but don't allow a film buildup (Tanacoat is brilliant)
- Fasten from underneath if at all possible, and
- Get as much airflow at the joist/decking interface as possible (my patented profile does this)

Stump Caps

A friend recently had a problem with termites in some house stumps as illustrated above. Fortunately there was no damage done to the building which was saved by the stump caps. The caps don't stop infection but, to gain entry to the building, the termites have to leave the centre of the post and build a very obvious mud bridge over the cap - on the right image you can see where this was done. Check annually to ensure there are no problems.

Problems arose when builders used to drive a clout through the cap to keep it in place and then the cap rusted around the nail.

Case History - RothoBlass Headquarters, Italy
This project uses Cross Laminated Timber

My new book, Timber Joints, contains a number of case histories and here is a particularly interesting one involving cross laminated timber (CLT). I am impressed with the range of connectors available from Rothoblaas.

Rothoblass headquarters Cortaccia Italy.

Inside the warehouse

Exterior of building showing cantilevered roof.

The former headquarters of Rothoblaas was a conventional building but when the time came to build a new headquarters in Cortaccia, Northern Italy, the opportunity arose to construct a structure showing the use of modern fasteners and membranes in the construction of large timber buildings. By using standard Rothoblaas product throughout it allowed an easy reference point for the history and performance of all the structural products. The building was designed with the architectural intent of reflecting the main activity of Rothoblaas in the form of a box of screws.

CLT connection at Rothoblaas headquarters. CLT connection at Rothoblaas headquarters.

The envelope of the rectangular building, constructed in three stages between 2004 and 2016 utilises glass on two sides and CLT panels on the other sides. European softwood is used throughout combined with steel columns, some of which are concrete filled for fire resistance. The softwood glue laminated beams are connected with Rothoblaas's own Alubrackets which are a concealed connector. The method of fixing the CLT panels allows the dismantling and reassembly with future expansion.

The facade is mostly clad with vertical wood, Also utilised are Rothoblaas membranes which gives a deeper effect of the facade. The roof is plain and on the south side overhangs 5 m past the wall like an open screw box which allows light in winter and reduces heat in summer. The roof also supports 1000 m2 of solar panels which supply 80% of the energy needed for lighting (LED), power, cooling and warming.

April 2017

Did I See the Monstrosity in Barcaldine?
How Not to Install a Post
Sons of Gwalia Headframe Restoration
I'd Give that Landing 5 out of 10

Did I See the Monstrosity in Barcaldine?

Recently I spent a few days in Longreach, 12 hours driving from Gatton. My hosts asked, "Did I see the monstrosity in Barcaldine?" I knew what they meant, the Tree of Knowledge Memorial. I replied that to me it was beautiful. I suppose we all recognise good functionality but beauty really is in the eye of the beholder. This particular structure is extremely well executed and a credit to all involved. The details of the memorial are included in my book *Architectural Timber Battens*.

Just a tip - some local wag left a nut and washer on the ground under the memorial which led to a frantic search to determine which of the hanging 125x125 pieces was about ready to impale a tourist. After a major inspection job they find out that all the nuts were in place. Using a characteristic nut (like a Glenlock) would be worth doing. It would spoil the local's fun though.

How Not to Install a Post

In my book *The Seven Deadly Sins of External Timber Design* I have a section about how to insert a hardwood post in the ground - it is different to pine. Frankly, I never addressed the one thing I thought it would ever be necessary to address. That is, be careful where you actually put the post. Power poles in the middle of the road are a common feature of Longreach. I am told the tourists go around the outside and the locals go on the inside. Inattentive or inebriated locals and tourists may choose a different path.

Sons of Gwalia Headframe Restoration Options
(Not a paid Advertisement)

This month I had hoped to bring you a report of a prefabricated library built in the Solomon Islands by my good friend Dr. Dan Tingley. The building utilises large dimension timber and is probably the best library in that nation. Hopefully I can bring you this story next month. Instead, Dan helped me by providing a copy of the proposal by Timber Restoration Systems for the restoration of the Sons of Gwalia headrig near Leonora in Western Australia which is built from Douglas Fir (Oregon). Below I have condensed and reformatted the report. I mentioned this historic structure a few months back when I wrote about the 100 year life achieved by non-durable timber in a dry climate.

The problem that led to the need for restoration

Fungi are the most common form of wood deterioration but, to become active, they need favourable conditions which are:

- moderate temperature (between 5C and 50C)
- oxygen (above 21%), and;
- moisture content of approximately 20% or greater

The environment around Leonora has limited rainfall which, more than anything, explains why so many elements in the old structure made with low durability untreated Douglas fir are still in good condition. In these environments, dew, rather than rain, can become the primary cause of decay and degradation as it condenses around metal fasteners localising moisture content to above 20% (into the decay zone). Decay or loss of specific gravity is usually found in these locations and this is the case with the Gwalia headrig.

Another cause of degrade to the structure is due to corrosion of the bolts leading to ferric ions from rusting metal fasteners migrating into the wood. This in turn leads to embrittlement of the lignin in the wood which in time results in the wood shrinking away from the metal fastener causing the structure to become loose and sloppy. Fortunately, the sons of Gwalia mine is in an area where there is low embedded corrosion which explains why the black steel fasteners have also lasted a long time.

After 100 years of exposure both these forms of attack have taken their toll and the historic structure needs to be restored. A previous study indicated that 56 members needed to be replaced.

Restoration options

The primary objective of the restoration is to recreate a structure that has been in existence for over a hundred years. The first option was to disassemble and reconstruct the structure with 50% of the elements being replaced with new karri (more than previously assessed). The second option is to disassemble the old structure and rebuild using all new pressure treated douglas fir (100 year life), sourced from the same location as it was originally found in Oregon. Another option (2A) involves utilizing douglas fir for the replacement elements instead of karri. The cost increase to use douglas fir versus karri is 3% and not a factor in the total scope of the job.

The total cost of Option One for the dismantlement and reconstruction with new karri elements would be $699,258. The total cost of this option with douglas fir replacement elements is $723,646. The total cost of a greenfield approach is $611,933 which includes only new treated Douglas Fir elements. See summary table below of the various option costs.

BREAKDOWN OF TENDER SUM	Option 1	Option 2A	Option 2B
Preliminaries	$ 78,737	$ 92,070	$112,100
Deconstruction	$226,000	$226,000	$ 96,000
Reconstruction	$308,953	$317,790	$308,203
Provisional and Monetary Sums: Galvanised Metal Fasteners	$ 20,000	$ 20,000	$ 40,000
Repairs to scarf splice and disconnected brace ends	$ 2,000	$ 2,000	
Value of Work	$635,689	$657,860	$556,303
GST	$ 63,569	$ 65,786	$ 55,630
TENDER SUM	$699,258	$723,646	$611,933

The heritage value of retaining some of the old elements is important but that comes with a price as the labor cost in reusing it will overwhelm the cost savings of the wood. It is estimated that it would take an estimated 700 hours of labor to reclaim wood from this structure. The look of old and new wood would be obvious but a judicial reuse of the more robust and attractive elements could preserve the look and feel of the old structure with more new elements allowing less time for disassembly and for reassembly. If in fact the timber materials were not to be saved and a new structure with all new douglas fir would be utilized then the cost of disassembly is much lower.

Should some of the old untreated timbers be reused, Dr. Tingley also recommended diffusing the timbers with sodium borate salt rods to extend their life. The treatment holes can be hidden as much as possible and wood bungs can be installed in the drilled holes so they do not detract from the look of the headframe.

If I am reading the Leonora Council minutes right, the tender appears to be let to another company for almost double the price quoted by Timber Restoration Systems. And you ever wonder why I thought it was easier being a consultant and a landlord instead of a business owner!

I'd Give That Landing 5 out of 10

Flying back from some work in Sydney on Qantas I had a particularly rough landing in Brisbane. The two retired headmasters I was sitting next to said, "I would give that landing a 5 out of 10," I reminded them that landings are not graded, they are either Pass or Fail. The remains of a Qantas fail can be seen at the Founders Museum in Longreach. Timber durability is somewhat similar. People think of the numbers 1 to 4 as hard categories and all the species in that group are the same all performing equally, much like a pass or fail landing. It is better to think of them not as hard values but as a sliding scale. A species might be a durability class 2 in ground but might be very close to being a one or at the other end, a three.

An example is cypress which I always knew to be a durability 1 in ground but is now classed as a durability 2. It's not that it's durability has dropped dramatically over a few years, it always has been hovering on the margin of one and two. I have also seen durability 2 changed to a 3. it would have been hovering at the bottom margin. Now clearly, if the timber is exposed to the weather above ground or in ground, you are not going to get the same performance from all durability class 2 timbers. In fact one study showed that there could be almost 50% difference in life expectancy between the bottom end of Durability class 2 in ground and the top end. The lesson: do your homework and be aware that when you go beyond the old proven royal species you are taking risks.

Edgar Stubbersfield

May 2017

This Timber Library is Cyclone and Earthquake Resistant
Jack's Rant About Dodgy Treatment
When is H3 not H3
Everything You need to Know About Timber Joints

This Timber Library is Cyclone and Earthquake Resistant
Not a paid advertisement

General layout of the building.
The Longer and More Interesting Baptist Version of the story

Kia is a remote village of about 2500-3000 on the northern tip of Santa Isabel. It is an island of rusted Japanese machine gun nests that overlooked the great World War 2 battle of Guadalcanal. The village has no power apart from some 12 volt solar panels, no motor vehicles nor running water. The village is so remote that It is only serviced fortnightly by a ship from Honiara. The trip takes anything from 22 to 30 hours, depending on the sea conditions, the number of passengers and the amount of cargo. The school in Kia had 500 students (but really needed to service 1000) from kindergarten to grade 6 but it was barely functioning and in danger of closing completely. As it only operated half a day it could only provide a grade 3 or grade 4 education at best. The island of Santa Isabel has some of the lowest literacy rates in the Solomon Islands.

Three years ago, women and teachers from Kia came on an acapella singing tour to Australia. It was hoped that they might raise funds to support their school. As fate would have it, the large church they were scheduled to sing in at Redcliffe cancelled so, at the last minute, the pastor at the small Deception Bay Baptist let them come to that church instead. That night they just happened to meet my friend Dr. Dan Tingley who thought their singing was heavenly! They shared with him that they had received a container of books from a church school that had closed but as their library was not climate controlled the books will quickly be destroyed. All the other existing buildings were also dilapidated.

Further, apart from the limited education that could be provided, the children had to leave their parents to go to Honiara when they went into grade 7. Unfortunately there was then a significant risk of falling into the sex trafficking industry. (The Solomons are rated as a mid-tiered nation as far as risk.) Dr. Dan suggested they apply to the Tingley Family Foundation board for funding for the library. This project met one of the boards objectives which was, to help prevent child sex trafficking. They applied for funding for a spacious climate controlled library and were approved.

Unfortunately, it then took three years to get government approvals and land title and commitment from the Chiefs in the village of Kia to not convert the building to some other use than education and library. The design was completed by February 2016. From March to October that year it was prefabricated and then assembled then dissembled at the facilities of **Wood Research and Development** in Jefferson, Oregon and shipped out in four containers.

When the kit arrived, the large bearers were used as paddle boards and paddled across the water from the ships. It then took 30 villages to carry them up to the top of the hill!!! Under great hardship and tough conditions the large fully contained library was built on a hill top in a very remote jungle location. Work and witness crews from two churches in Oregon and also Deception Bay Baptist Church plus a team of paid professionals from **Timber Restoration Services** started assembling the library in November 2016. The whole Tingley family went over and Dr. Dan described it as "probably the most interesting experience of our life as a family." The building was completed except for few last details in February/March 2017. Opening of this library, with a commercial value of about $700,000 $US is July 2017.

Without any extra funding being forthcoming from the Solomon Island Government, the team agreed to supply all the funds necessary to add a year each year to the school, starting this year with grade 7. It will eventually cater from Kindergarten to Grade 12. This means children will no longer will have to go to Honiara so fulfilling the goals of the foundation.

As for the building itself, it is a complete engineered wood building including the structural insulated panels and is believed to be the best Library for children in the Solomons. The Oregon bearers are treated with oil based copper napthenate, with the treatment done after all cutting and drilling has been done. The structure has a design life of 100 years in the jungle. The bearers are so large because the design load for a library is very high – books are heavy!

The library is totally self-contained and climate controlled, with a large solar power system. The dehumidifier and AC unit only run for 30 minutes to bring the big cavity down to target RH and temp levels. Included in the fit out were large screen flat TVs, components for teaching, desks chairs for three teachers and benches and tables for 100 students at a time and room for all the books that was contained in one large container. The building is not just designed for library occupancy loads but also for 190 kpm winds making it a safe shelter now for the village (note the concrete columns). It is also designed to withstand an earthquake up to 7.6 magnitude. An earthquake hit the week after the building was finished with no damage.

The story is one of courage and commitment from all who contributed. Praise God that he allowed us to be involved. The work has not stopped. There are several smaller construction projects that will be taking place around the island. It is planned to make improvements to elderly housing, the single medical clinic on the island and work to improve the living condition of those will special needs.

Much good has come above because of this building. The seed sown has multiplied many times over already. As Dr. Dan says "Any naysayers will just have to come and help the kids out at the Solomons and see the face of Jesus in every little girl's face that gets saved from child prostitution."

Want to be part of future assistance to the school at Kia, you can do this two ways

1. By donating through the **Tingley Family Foundation Kia Project**
2. By volunteering to help as they do other projects like a medical clinic.

For my Baptist readers, yes, I have interests outside of timber. You might find these three books of interest, the first two are sermons I and other laymen have preached in our little Baptist church in the middle of a potato field at Tenthill Queensland. The third contains documents I edited that were written by Herman Windolf, the first ordained German Baptist pastor in Queensland. It tells of his journey to Australia by clipper ship in the 1870's and then his journey from Brisbane to Kalbar and the start of his ministry. For all readers, Baptist to atheist, it is fascinating reading and will give you a newfound respect for our pioneers. The Emigration Museum in Hamburg said "We are working on emigration to Australia at the moment and that is just perfect showing what exactly it was like in those days."

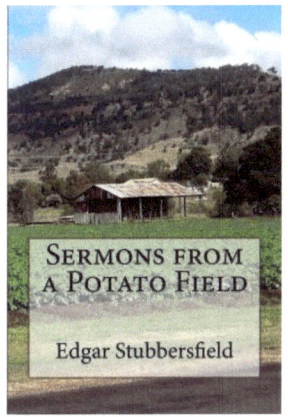
Sermons from a Potato Field

Lettuce Pray – More Sermons from a Potato field

Herman Windolf and the Queensland German Baptists

The opportunities for similar buildings in remote parts of Australia are obvious. Contact Dan Tingley 0467 625 926 or Stephen Richards 0428 983 328 to discuss your needs.

Jack Has a Rant About Dodgy Treatment

Jack's Norton's "rant" below is from the May edition of *Contact*, the Newsletter of the Timber Preservers Association. [Reprinted with permission.] A little about Jack - Jack Norton is a legend among timber preservers. When we Queenslanders had a Timber Utilisation and Marketing Act, Jack was the one who ensured that we did the right thing and would have prosecuted us if we stepped out of line. With nicknames of Captain Chaos and Captain Preservation none of us were game enough to step out of line, besides he was too nice a person to want to upset. Then one of our political masters noticed that there had not been a prosecution under the Act so decided we didn't need its protection. Without Acts (NSW did the same) and policemen, timber treatment standards from some suppliers have slipped badly. Politicians, and we trust them to run our state and country!

Images of badly treated sleepers taken from resellers websites, they think they are good Just a tip, the dark bits are the areas that are treated, should be 80% of the cross section.

Jack's rant here - It never ceases to amaze me that our industry finds it so hard to comply with treatment specifications – at least for landscaping products. Perhaps we should give up and stop calling palings and landscape sleepers 'preservative treated'.

A couple of weeks ago, my daughter asked for help to level out the ground under her clothes line. Her clothes line is about 4m long and is one of those pull out things rather than a rotator. The plan was to dig into the slope along one length and use the spoil to raise the opposite side. This needed a small retaining wall down one side.

The son in-law and I dutifully headed off to the local hardware house (guess who??) and this is where the rant comes in. After a short lesson in sapwood/heartwood and preservative penetration, we sorted through two packs of landscape sleepers and found two (yes, two) that I thought had a chance of meeting the penetration specifications in the Standard. We needed eight.

I admit that sleepers and palings are low value low cost products, but the punters out there expect them to perform and there are an awful lot of them pouring into the market place. I regularly get queries about the performance of landscape sleepers and part of the advice is that if the wall is more than 1m high then H5 treated sleepers should be used. This is a requirement of the BCA. The only problem with this advice is . . . . 'where do you buy H5 sleepers' ???????

I am seeing increasing availability of non-timber sleepers which cost a hell of a lot more than the timber product but are obviously being sold. Otherwise the hardware shop(s) wouldn't stock them. You have to ask why the punters are prepared to pay more and the only reason I can think of is reliability!

As always, I am open to hear from you as to how we might lift our game.

Ted's rant here - While the roundwood market suffered serious decline, the overall market for H3-H5 timber doubled between 2001-2011 and there are many markets, new and traditional, that could open up or return to timber. But if we cant get the basics right the market will collapse just as quickly as it grew. Talk to me about your specifications. Simon T, you need to talk to me.

When is H3 not H3?

The definition of H3 treatment from AS1604.1 is "outside, above ground, subject to periodic moderate wetting and leaching." Suitable applications given in the standard are fascia, pergolas, windows, framing and decking. It was pointed out to me recently that one supplier of H3 LVL says on their literature *"LOSP H3 Not recommended for use in external, exposed applications unless installed with effective moisture protection."* Compare that with the standard's definition of H2, "Inside, above ground protected from wetting and no leaching." Applications are framing used in dry situations.

Well I suppose I studied too much philosophy where importance is given to the meaning of words but quite frankly, I cannot see too much difference between the suppliers permitted "H3" use and the formal definition of H2.

H3 is H3 but perhaps Jack nailed it on the head in the previous article. Would I use an LVL when very durable hardwoods are readily available? No I wouldn't. Would I trust a treatment certificate? It depends on who's it is. But don't let me discourage you.

June 2017

How to Protect and Keep Your Deck Looking Good
Joining Decking on Commercial Decks
Timber Sound Sculptures

How to Protect and Keep Your Deck Looking Good
By Steven Koch (with slight tweaks by me)

Steven Koch is the Key Account & Fire Retardant Manager with Lonza Wood Protection and has been a friend for many years now. In a former life he was a surface coatings R&D chemist and, on starting with Lonza, developed *Tanacoat*, a penetrating oil decking finish, for my company. It is a product I believe in.

Introduction

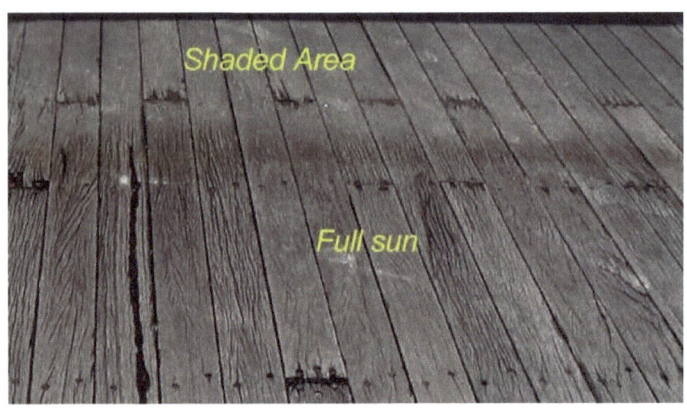

The image shows an old weather exposed deck where part is shaded but not covered. Every bit of appropriate protection you give your deck makes a big difference. Image courtesy Timber Queensland

I have only oiled my covered ironbark deck once since 1992 when I built the house but a weather exposed deck requires far more care than one that is under a roof. After all, you've invested money, time and effort into your deck so it is important to protect it and keep it looking its best as long as possible. Fortunately, it's fairly simple and cost-effective to do this if you follow our guidelines which are, to use a deck cleaner (and possibly a restorer as well) and apply Tanacoat once a year. Personally, I would not substitute with another product. The use of a deck restorer may be needed as it can bring your deck it back to its former glory before you use Tanacoat. But let me stress, that while there are things that you should do, there are also things that you should not do. We will look at both.

The things you should do

Maintaining your deck

Using a deck cleaner to remove moss, mould, algae and general grease and dirt will make your deck look much cleaner and brighter. Try and do this at least once a year.

Step 1. First, remove any loose or large accumulations of moss or algae with a stiff brush or scraper, then brush off any general loose debris from the deck. Prepare deck cleaner solution according to the instructions on packaging, and then apply it to the deck using a brush, sprayer or watering can with a rose.

Step 2. Scrub the surface immediately with a stiff brush after you've put on the cleaner, and leave it to stand.

Step 3. Rinse off thoroughly with clean water using a hose, ensuring you've washed all residues away. Allow your deck to dry before you apply Tanacoat. Drying time will vary depending on weather conditions.

How to restore your deck

Once you have cleaned your deck, if it has turned grey or looks a bit weathered, you can put on a deck restorer to return it to its original colour before applying Tanacoat. **Top tip -** When you use deck restorer, work on small manageable areas at a time (3-4 deck boards) so you can finish your application, scrubbing and rinsing within 15 minutes. **Safety first -** If you're using a pressure washer, make sure you wear safety goggles to protect your eyes from any flying fragments. Note: Some people go straight to the restoration system without cleaning first. If the deck is very dirty this can lead to a blotchy result.

Step 1. First, use a stiff brush to remove loose debris, and take off any moss, mould and algae with a pressure washer. Make sure the surface is bare, and that you've removed any existing coating or stain before you start putting on the deck restorer solution. **Note:** some commercial pressure washers have far more power than a domestic unit and can damage the timber, particularly softwood. Do a small trial first. Pressure washers should only be used infrequently and vary carefully.

Step 2. Apply deck restorer solution to your deck with a brush.

Step 3. Immediately after you've applied the deck restorer solution, work it into the surface of the wood with a scrubbing pad or stiff brush. Then leave it to stand a short time but do not allow to dry.

Step 4. Rinse off thoroughly with clean water using a hose or watering can, ensuring you've washed away all the residues. Allow time for your deck to dry out completely before you apply Tanacoat. Drying time will vary depending on weather conditions.

Applying Tanacoat

Tanacoat can be applied much like any other decking oil using a brush, roller or lambs wool applicator. It is important that it is not applied too thickly and that any excess Tanacoat on the surface must be removed. A number of light coats is better than one heavy coat as this avoids areas where the Tanacoat just sits on the surface. As with image in Step 4 above, work to boards to avoid overlaps.

The Things You Should Not Do

Film finishes are not the answer as they can promote decay

Your deck is nicely cleaned and/or restored but you have doubts about using Tanacoat. Why should you when there are far more expensive gloss film finishes available from big name manufacturers. Surely they have to be better. Well no. A film finish is likely to promote decay. When there is a break in the surface coating, moisture enters and is trapped underneath and decay can result, as it did with the highly durable spotted gum in the images above. If you are not on top of your film coating's maintenance you may find also that you have to sand between coats.

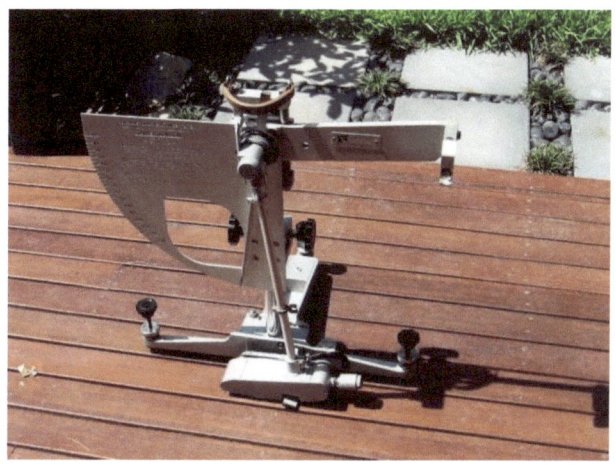

Probably the biggest consideration is slip resistance. When I tested the slip resistance of a wet film finish on a dressed shotedge deck the results were that it was highly likely that someone would slip. By contrast, *Deckwood* lightly sanded and oiled with Tanacoat went R12.

The other consideration is pressure washing which has been mentioned above. It should be very infrequent and careful. Tanacoat can be purchased from Outdoor Structures Australia. Call Tammy on 0403 601 041

Joining Decking on Commercial Decks

The consequence of not planning how you will join your decking!

Building decks are complicated as, usually, decking needs to be joined. All to often, no thought is given to how you join the decking. The builder purchases say 1000 metres of decking and just butts it up on a 50 mm joist. "I have been building decks for 20 years," he will say but, in reality, he has been building decks badly for 20 years. The screws and resultant splitting on the image on the left says it all, and that is on a 75 mm joist! The ends are butted together, which holds moisture which in turn readily enters the end grain and decay results.

Building commercial decks with lineal decking and face fixings simply does not work if you want a trouble free deck that reaches its maximum possible life. The designer of this deck I saw in York UK recognised the problem and tried to sort it by overhanging about 220 mm and connecting the ends of the decking with wooden dowels. I would not say a complete success. Our Australian climate would quickly see decay where the dowel enters the end grain. There has to be a better way. At least better for the asset owner, though it involves more trouble for the designer and care in ordering material by the builder.

The right and wrong way to do it

The only way that you can effectively face fix decking is to use set length decking and design where the joins are placed, which of course you should stagger. Now getting back to those builders who have been building decks badly for 20 years. The image on the left is on a deck designed by my old company. The builder who was very capable and conscientious followed the detail provided on how to join the decking. There are two joists with about a 150 mm gap between them. The deck overhangs about 75 mm and there is about a 5 mm gap between the boards to stop moisture entering through the end grain. The image on the right was by a company that invariably ignored specifications and construction details. Mercifully they are no longer trading but there are plenty more where they came from. They used a double joist all right but had no idea what they were doing. What a waste. Note the dreaded film finish also.

It is not hard to do the join correctly. I describe it in detail in my book *Deck and Boardwalk Design Essentials*. You really shouldn't be designing a deck without inwardly digesting my guide and following the design check list. There are things that you do with timber at your peril just like any other material.

Kim Bowman Music
Not a paid commercial

Sound sculptures using Lockyer Valley ironbark

When I was trading, I used to supply Kim Bowman with the ironbark he needed for his sound sculptures. I am pleased to see that he is still purchasing his ironbark from another Lockyer Valley mill, Muckerts Sawmill. We used to take it year about to win the quality awards so he is in good hands. Happy to give you a mention Kim.

July 2017

A Reminder about Pine
Choosing Timber by Colour - a Lesson from Japan
City of Gold Coast Builds an Outstanding Deck
What Decking Profile is That

A Reminder About Pine

Decay in an originally pink primed pine post

Decay in roof beam

The two images above are from a recent consultancy where I was asked to advise what was happening to 13 year old pine that was only being held together by the paint. The thing is, it was not all decaying and the post and beam next to failed members might be perfectly sound. When the correct level of preservative chemical is used, and appropriate building practices are also used, timber treatments work well but they only work on sapwood, whether it be pine or hardwood. The failed pieces simply had insufficient sapwood and should never have been sold as "treated". Untreatable heartwood should not make up more than 20% of the cross section. How do you know how much preservative is present when it is pink primed and especially if a clear LOSP is used?

If I had a project which had to succeed, I would require the pine to be preconditioned, incised to a depth of 10 mm and treated preferably to H4. The incising process allows the chemicals to penetrate the heartwood and the extra chemical cost for H4 is not significant when weighed against the cost of failure. Unfortunately, no one is supplying timber to this specification and there are only two incisors in the country. Until such material is available, I would recommend that you use royal species hardwood over pine for external timber structures.

My guide will assist you to understand more about timber preservation.

Choosing Timber by Colour - A Lesson from Japan

Decay in Jarrah in Japan

Jarrah replaced with plastic

Specifying timber to achieve the colour you want can lead to very unsatisfactory results. Let me explain. In the past I sent a lot of spotted gum to Japan and was proud to be part of projects with aesthetics, the likes of which I had not seen in Australia. The landscape architects were fearless in spending their client's money but in return delivered projects that were outstanding. The was one criticism I was constantly receiving was that my spotted gum was not red!

The Japanese love the colour red and because of that, job after job was going to Jarrah from Western Australia and for no other reason than it was red. Then the failures started. An example is the the Takashimaya Boardwalk project in Shinjuku, Tokyo illustrated above (since largely demolished and replaced with plastic). The boards were placed without gaps and despite shrinkage the gaps filled up causing water to form puddles (some quite large) on the decking on rainy days. (This is not a problem with Deckwood) Also, at times, poorer quality Jarrah was used. It all but killed the export of Australian hardwood to Japan.

Now for many Japanese specifiers, all Australian timbers were labelled with the same brush as jarrah. I have featured the work of Kurata Co a number of times, a Japanese company specialising is well built spotted gum structures in Japan. Kurata Co did not want to hear the word Jarrah associated with Eucalypts at all since it had such a bad image in Japan — its poor performance exacerbated by the poor way it was installed. In the end a once lucrative market has had to be slowly re-established.

On dressed timber, Tanacoat with a suitable stain goes part way towards getting the colour you want

City of Gold Coast Builds an Outstanding Deck

Asset Owner: City Of Gold Coast
Location: Southport Broadwater Parklands
Engineers: Aecom
Prime Contractor: Glascott Civil
Carpenter: Top Knot Carpentry
Senior timber Consultant: Ted Stubbersfield

The City of Gold Coast wanted to build a high quality, trouble free deck in one of their premier parks, Broadwater Parklands at Southport. The deck is intended to play a part in the upcoming Commonwealth Games but they were apprehensive as, like many authorities, they were having difficulty with the great variability of timber decks and boardwalks. Unlike some others, however, the City was also aware that alternatives to timber had as many if not more problems. I was asked by Major Projects, Economic Development and Major Projects Directorate if I could assist the City with their problem.

I suggested that they inspect the deck we detailed and supplied at Calypso Bay at Jacobs Well as you can't build a better deck than that and, being well over ten years old, they could see how well a deck should age. It was told that, despite the deck being 7.2 metres wide and 450 metres long, there was only one board that was commented on. After establishing timber can meet the City's expectation, I followed that with CPD sessions on timber design to raise awareness of external timber issues and then a number of my technical guides were purchased.

The specification for Deckwood was followed along the need for wide joists and designing the join. Critically, on my advice they ensured that every piece of timber was inspected for compliance to grade. We assisted at every stage of this project which involved looking at the plans (the Devil is in the detail), inspecting construction, grading some of the hardwood and giving a final inspection. Most importantly, I believe that, with a more complete understanding of the issues, knowing where to obtain good design information and having checklists, this standard of timber structure is achievable every time going on into the future. As this project demonstrates, having knowledge of how timber operates in an outdoor environment, employing good design, quality materials and quality construction processes ensures a successful outcome.

Top marks to the City of Gold Coast for being proactive about raising standards. It is worth driving to the site to have a good look. For more information about this outstanding project contact Jeremy Hall, Principal Project Officer for the deck.

What Decking Profile is That

Decking image from last month's newsletter

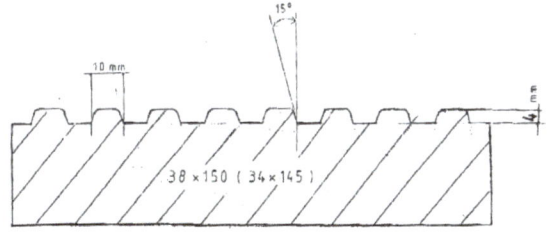
Detail of the profile

One of my readers asked me what the profile was in last month's newsletter about deck maintenance. It is very common in the UK and is used as an anti-slip product. I looked at it years ago and considered it would be unsuitable for Australian conditions as the top is dressed and moisture will sit in the grooves. These two factors lead to premature degrade.

I my experience the best profile for external decking is Deckwood as it has a rough sawn face for durability and slip resistance, and a cross section designed to give maximum air flow.

August 2017

Important Changes to Consultancy Arrangements
It Seemed a Good Idea At the Time
Something Else That Seemed A Good Idea
Wood Encouragement Policy - A Mixed Blessing?
Mareeba Shire Turns to Timber Bridges over Concrete

Important Changes to Consultancy Arrangements

I am pleased to advise that I am now a Senior Timber Consultant with the leading firm of durability consultants, BCRC (www.bcrc.com.au). The BCRC team is led by some of the most well know people in the construction materials area, Frank Papworth, Bob Munn and Marton Marosszeky. It is an honour to have my knowledge recognised by such people.

BCRC assist with specifying materials for new projects that will be durable or assessing existing structures to determine their state of deterioration, why materials used were not durable and how to rectify the issue using materials or protection systems that will be durable. By linking with BCRC, my timber services can be integrated with a wide range of international technical experts specialising in different fields of construction materials, including concrete, steel, coatings, brickwork and others. Overall, we are able to bring to bear the most up to date thinking from some of the best minds in the world. This combines with unsurpassed experience and state-of-the-art diagnostic equipment to give leading support.

The new arrangements are:

- Where there are existing arrangements – No change
- Smaller or simpler consultancies, I will still deal direct
- All larger or complex consultancies will be through BCRC
- All Expert Witness work will be through BCRC

With offices in most states, you should look no further than BCRC when you need a Durability Consultant.

It Seemed a Good Idea at the Time

Let me tell you a sad story: recently I replaced the roof of our home. Back in 1992 when I built our home I decided to use a new product called Lysaght Coolclad roofing instead of tried and tested colorbond. The foil backing was marketed as an effective insulation and I thought I was very clever to use it. That was until a couple of years ago when I started to get some mould on the inside of the house. The plumber had bad news, the end of all the sheets were badly rusted and I needed a new roof and of course the warranty had expired. Moisture had entered between the foil and the sheet and rust ensued.

What I see of timber substitutes, such as plastic and composite decking, seems to me to be in much the same category of seeming a good idea at the time. Like my iron, the runs simply aren't on the board yet and I have seen enough to believe that when used correctly, royal species Australian hardwood is still the best answer for external timber applications. The image shows how fire has affected a plastic deck. I urge you to be cautious when considering timber alternatives.

Something Else That Seemed a Good Idea
(or Treat End Grain With Respect)

Decorative ball on top of post

Resultant decay

The repair   End grain opening up

If you have attended My CPD session on *Utilising Heart In Timber* you would have learnt the difference between two very confusing terms, heartwood and wood with heart. What we are looking at here is the end grain of heartwood and the images show why you need to treat it with respect. Also, if you are going to make a mistake, at least do it on your own home, not a client's.

My home is a reproduction pre-federation Queenslander. I thought it would be a nice idea to dress up the posts with decorative timber balls. I drilled into the tops of the posts and glued them in. No problem on the back steps on the northern side (see the first top image) but as for the front steps, it was a disaster (second top image). The handrails are fitted close to the top of the posts so this decay very nearly cost me a complete rebuild of my front stairs. Fortunately I was able to cap them in time.

The fourth image shows the top of the stairs on the eastern side which were not "dressed up" and you can see how 25 years of exposure to the elements has caused the end gran to open. Most of the time it was unpainted. Moisture enters the end grain 8 times faster than through the side grain. I should have just put a sloping top on all the posts. There is no problem with balls in the internal steps but then there is no weather to deal with.

I had planned to reprint an article from Roads and Civil Works Australia entitled *Timber Bridge Renewal and Repair: A Renewed Focus* but it was too long. I have selected portions of it and abridged it (and added a bit in the section below) It is very worthwhile reading as it touches the whole subject of timber use, particularly its environmental credentials, not just bridges. *This article appeared in the June/July issue of Roads & Civil Works Australia and is republished with the publisher's permission.*

A Wood Encouragement Policy - A Mixed Blessing?

An atrocious plastic bollard   An equally atrocious timber bollard

Dr Dan Tingly, the timber bridge expert (and a valued close friend) commented, "We've talked to some council representatives who went through three courses each for concrete and steel (12-13 weeks per course), compared to two weeks of timber design in a materials class. This lack of training and understanding has them discarding or passing over timber options in favour of steel and concrete as they get into the work force."

Corresponding to a decreasing knowledge of timber, there is an increasing trend by governments globally to adopt a wood encouragement policy (WEP), which requires timber to be considered the preferred construction material in projects when it is equally fit-for-purpose. "Within Australia, 12 councils across four states have already adopted a WEP, including Fraser Coast and Gympie Councils, who became the first councils in [Queensland] to do so.

(Ted's comment from here) While it is a positive move I fear that it could be counterproductive without an increase in timber knowledge. As much as I love timber, a poorly designed, supplied and constructed timber structure ultimately hurts our industry, not assists it. We can't even get simple things right. I supplied 1200 timber bollards to one local government back in 2012. Someone in that authority, not understanding what he/she was looking at, about a year after installation thought they needed to be oiled and then came to the conclusion that timber represented an unacceptable maintenance burden and swung that council on to plastic bollards. But plastic had already failed, as per the image of the 10 year old bollard above which needed a star picket to hold it together. It is not hard for appropriate timber to hold its own against this product.

One of my 30 year old bollards writes off a car and protects a playground
(bent cross member, radiator into engine)

For the next large bollard project, that council reverted to timber but used landscaping sleepers with the heart in the centre which will not age gracefully. See the image beside the plastic bollard above. How do you ever get that council to consider timber again?

Good intentions must also be backed up with increased knowledge, appropriate specifications, and independent grade conformation. If you need assistance in this area I can offer training and consultancy services.

Mareeba Shire Turns to Timber Bridges over Concrete

Mareeba Shire Council, on the Atherton Tableland in Far North Queensland, has a mix of 20 timber and concrete bridges and like other councils "doesn't have the means to fund replacements," says Glenda Kirk, Contracts & Project Management Officer at Mareeba Shire Council. The council has recently begun a program of works to repair and renew three timber bridges on low-order roads. "If we were to put them under road project priorities, we'd never get them over the line," Ms Kirk says. Fortunately she had brought experiences and learnings in this area from her previous role with the Cassowary Coast Regional Council.

Ms. Kirk says the focus on timber bridge renewal rather than replacement proved effective and financially beneficial for Cassowary Coast, and the goal is to achieve the same at Mareeba. "The main thing about single-lane timber bridges is that the abutments will be fine, but the girders are what will be failing or inadequate. If you put a concrete deck on abutments that are built to support timber, you may possibly ruin the substructure by overloading it."

Rather than repairing or restoring the original timber structure, she says the common alternative here is often to replace the bridge entirely with concrete. However, for rural councils, such as Mareeba Shire Council, which have an extensive road network and low population base, it's not a cost-effective option. "One of the things that's driving councils back to timber is cost – the costs of renewing a timber bridge asset can be three to five times cheaper than replacing it entirely," explains Ms. Kirk.

She says that people realise timber bridge renewal is not the silver bullet and, like other treatments, doesn't last forever, but advancements in timber engineering are beginning to establish timber bridge renewal as a viable and cost-effective option.

Based on Timber Restoration Systems' own experience, Mr. Tingley says timber bridge treatments usually cost 80 per cent less than the estimated price to replace a structure with concrete. "The cost of typical restoration strategies can range down to $600 to $1200 per square metre versus a greenfield concrete bridge, which can cost up to $6000 per square metre, with typical costs being in the $3500-per-square-metre range. Even when the super and deck are gone, if the timber substructure can be saved it will lead to costs for restoration from $1800 to $2200 per square metre. This is much less than greenfield concrete costs.

September 2017

Be Careful With Ply Fences
Wood Encouragement Policy - What is needed
Cairns Regional Council sets the Standard for Preservation

Be Careful with Ply Fencing

When I was writing my book on timber fences, I asked the ply guru at Carter Holt Harvey (CHH) about their recommendations for the use of *Shadowclad* in fencing. There has certainly been plenty used for that application. I was told that they did not recommend that product for fencing! I saw the above ply fence recently which was not faring too well. It is branded CHH *Shadowclad* but to be fair to CHH its application does not bear even lip service to their technical guides, so the issue is not with the product. When used in accordance with the manufacturers recommendations it performs well.

While I am not saying, "Don't build a ply fence" I am saying, "Proceed with caution and obtain written guidelines from the manufacturer on how to use their product in that application." And when the builder substitutes make sure you get an updated guideline. Oh, and notice the dark stain, that does the ply no favours. Only use light pastel shades. I give some guidance in the use of ply in fences in my book.

Have you purchased a copy yet or are you trusting the lowest price contractor to continually bring in high standards using material with no specification?

Unfortunately, I do not have a close up image of a good ply fence. I am sure they exist.

Wood Encouragement Policy. What is needed

Image Courtesy Dr Dan Tingley, Wood Research and Development

Last month I wrote an article, A Wood Encouragement Policy, A Mixed Blessing. In it I argued that there is no point specifying timber if you are going to use it badly as it will be counterproductive in the long run. Eileen Newbury, National Marketing and Communications Manager for Forest and Wood Products Australia (FWPA) set me the challenge. It is easy to identify the problems but could I also identify some of the solutions. So here are my thoughts:

Appropriate standards. The requirements for a piece if timber that will work appropriately in a roof truss are very different to those for decking and are different again for a bollard and even for a boardwalk joist. So many designers can't see past numbers such as F14 or F17 and fail to understand that while it is critical for roof trusses it is virtually meaningless for external timber where durability becomes more important than strength. Fortunately, I developed these and can help you with them.

Design Checklists. Inexperienced designers etc. need to be able to quickly tap into the wisdom of the ages. The understanding of why the areas highlighted in a checklist are important will come in time. It is the same mistakes being repeated time and time again. My books *Timber Footbridges* and *Deck and*

Boardwalk Design Essentials give checklists to asses your design or a tender you have received. I doubt if they have been look at seriously by other than a handful of people. They could save you so much grief.

Educate yourself. Now there is no excuse for ignorance. FWPA run an excellent resource, the Wood Solutions Campus where you can learn what you need on different subjects at starter, intermediate and advanced level. For design professionals who need more knowledge there is the Graduate Certificate in Timber (GradCert Timber) run by the University of Tasmania.

Scrap self-regulation of suppliers. I remember a time when under the Queensland Hardwood Quality Control scheme our grading was verified four times a year and likewise our timber preservation was also inspected four times a year. Branded timber actually meant something. That is all gone and with it the integrity of certificates supplied by some suppliers. One industry leader told me that grading back then was "bad" as the timber being supplied was too good!

Only deal with trained/experienced suppliers. When you go to a big box for your advice the danger is the salesman was selling ladies shoes the week before and has that most dangerous of things, a little knowledge. See Jack's Rant in the May Newsletter.

Don't choose your consultants on price. You need to ensure that your consultant has the necessary expertise in timber, or at least can tap into that expertise. My own observation is that the external use of timber can be more of an art than a science but it is not a dark art. It is all very logical.

Independently verify. What is so perverse about timber that you do not independently verify that the timber being supplied is what has been asked for. You do it with concrete!! One grader from NSW told me that he regularly rejects between 30-50% of timber presented for grading. I rejected 50% on a recent job. Some projects also require independent confirmation of treatment (see the next article). I can't stress how important independent verification is. Verification of treatment is more an issue with pine and verification of grading is the big issue with hardwood.

Make use of me. I have tried to put down in writing what I have learnt over a lifetime. The guides I have written are very practical. Avail yourself of my CPD sessions, get me to check drawings, get me to check construction, get me to check grading. See the City of Gold Coast deck in the July newsletter.

Edgar Stubbersfield

Cairns Regional Council Sets the Standard for Preservation

A boardwalk at Cairns Botanical Gardens using Deckwood that is performing well.

The decision by the Cairns Regional Council to require independent verification of successful preservation of the timber for an important project was presented at a recent treatment workshop as the direction for the future. The seminar run by the newly created *National Centre for Timber Design Life and Durability* was entitled *Quality Control and Assurance for Wood Preservation: The Nordic and North American Schemes Quality control and assurance (QC/QA) schemes.* These are mature schemes that have been developed to ensure that treated wood products are fit for purpose. We certainly can learn from the Nordic and North American experiences and build a first class QC/QA scheme that will give retailers and consumers great confidence in the performance of treated wood. Sadly industry participation at the workshop was poor. See July's newsletter to understand why it is needed

The Centre is a strategic initiative of the industry group Forest & Wood Products Australia (FWPA), and is a partnership between industry, academia and government. and is based at the University of the Sunshine Coast. The Centre will initially focus its efforts on the development of evidence-based data, systems and tools to underpin consumer confidence in the performance of timber products. Over time, the Centre would also create world-leading predictive models to enable architects and building specifiers to more easily choose the appropriate timber products for specific end uses and tasks.

One of the key objectives of the Centre, headed up by Professor Philip Evans, is to train talented young people in the field because too many of us that promote timber are getting old. The Centre will have access to some of the brightest minds in the best universities in Australia and around the world.

Unfortunately it is very early in the organisation's life and the website is not up and running yet. I will send the link through when I have it

Two New CPD Subjects Being Developed

Image Dennis Clark Photography

I am working on two new CPD subjects, Timber 101 and Boardwalk Design. I gave them a dry run for a class of landscape architecture students at QUT recently. A bit more work is needed but they can be finalised very quickly if you would like to have a presentation at your office.

October 2017

Writing a Book on External Furniture
Is Recycled Timber Seasoned?
New Book on Plywood
Be Careful Choosing Your Species
Two New CPD Sessions

Writing a Book on External Furniture

External furniture is not always just about a couple of cheap barbecue tables but can involve a large amount of expensive, custom designed furniture. Recently I saw such a project that had gone very badly wrong. This has led me to start writing a book on weather exposed timber furniture as opposed to patio furniture. Every Landscape Architect in the country should purchase a copy but I expect to only sell 10 copies. Is it worth it? Financially, no. But as Prof. Marton Marosszeky, a Director of BCRC, the construction materials and durability consultants I now work with, said "I find that you learn a lot in the writing, and it builds your knowledge, so if you have the time I would go for it." I am also being encouraged by Ralph Bayley of Guymer Bailey Architects who has done some very impressive work with external furniture.

I am on the lookout for images and insights from my readers. Images I need are:

Badly weathered pine BBQ table
Badly weathered hardwood BBQ table
Failed glue joints
Decayed sapwood
Decay under film finish.

I also want to know if you have had experience with jarrah. Any images and comments related to this new book will be gratefully received.

Is Recycled Timber Seasoned?

 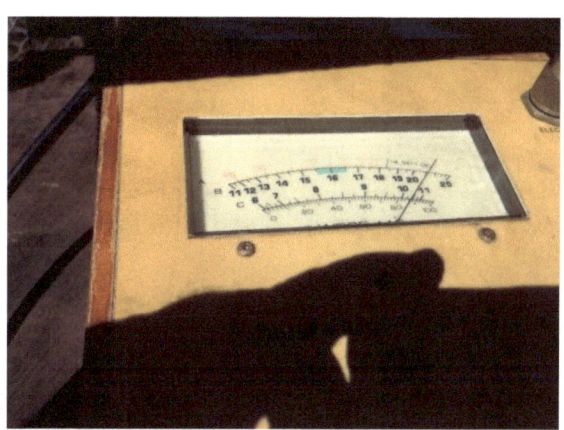

The short answer to the question about whether recycled timber is seasoned is, "You would not want to trust your professional indemnity to it. Take, for example, the 300x150 jarrah I inspected that had been in a wharf for over 50 years. The moisture content was constantly about 25% and timber does not start to shrink until it reaches this point and, as would be expected, they are still almost full size. The timber is simply too large to dry. If you took these pieces as is, gave them a wire brushing and then used them in some architectural feature they will give no problem.   But if you re-sawed them into 300x50 mm planks they would behave like green off saw timber and shrink the full 7.5% or almost 22 mm. This will cause problems when used for some structural purposes e.g. floor joists.

Conversely, if you take a 50 mm floor joist from a building, even just a couple of years old, and recycle it you will have no problems as far as shrinkage. (Serviceability is another matter though, it may have been in the building for 100 years but that does not mean it is a durable species that can be used externally.) But take timber from the larger sizes, re-saw it into say 25mm boards and produce dressed products from it and prepare yourself a claim. The image to the right shows recycled spotted gum which has shrunk so badly it that the shiplap is no longer lapping and you can see the insulation underneath.

So, proceed with caution. Specify and check your moisture contents when shrinkage is going to be an issue as with flooring, decking and cladding particularly.

New Book for Those Interested in Plywood

I know a few of my readers have a keen interest in plywood. A new book has been released entitled "A Guide to Manufacturing Rotary Veneer and Products from Small Logs". The book's editors are Bill Leggate, Robert McGarvin and Henri Bailleres of Forest Product Innovations, Salisbury Research Facility, Department of Agriculture and Fisheries, Queensland, Australia. The address is http://aciar.gov.au/files/mn182-.pdf

Figure 4.8. A 45 mm peeler core (left) produced from a spindleless veneer lathe, compared with a 130 mm peeler core produced from a standard, commercial spindled lathe.

One of the drivers behind this book was trying to find higher value products that could be produced from forest resources that were originally intended for woodchip. The big change has been the development of spindleless lathes that leave little more than a broom stick

A few days ago I called in to the Salisbury Research Facility to see Henri Bailleres and he showed me some of the latest things they were working on. One was this thick veneer produced from spotted gum billets ranging from 160-240 mm in diameter, material too small for sawmilling. Being French, Henri described this veneer as being the "crème de la crème" of veneers. He also used a bit of "French" to describe the difficulty in gluing it quickly but they are working on it.

Be Careful Choosing Your Species

The picture to the left is of 13 year old blackbutt used in a barbecue table in full sun. It is not aging gracefully. When you go away from the timbers that were traditionally used in an application and just go by a durability rating you can get this disappointing result. When writing to one timber merchant in Perth recently about jarrah, he commented *"It's funny you mention Colour, over here lighter wood preforms miserably in our climate, species like Selang batu twist and bow like you wouldn't believe, even the eastern states Blackbutt shrinks and checks like [not printable]."* So you can avoid issues like the one illustrated, the new book has a detailed specification for hardwood and pine [but a maintenance nightmare].

November 2017

Should Decks Be Load Limited?
It's a Good Idea to Pre-oil Your Decks
The Customer Isn't Always Right
Timber Garden Retaining Walls
Writing a book on External Furniture

Should Decks be Load Limited?

Last month, Geoff Stringer, The Product Development Manager at Hyne gave a presentation for Timber Queensland entitled *Reliably Durable Timber Structures from Treated Timber*. In it, he looks at the causes of deck failures and poses the question of whether decks should be load limited. I have known Geoff since 1984 when I was with Gatton Sawmilling Co. and he was with TRADAC. Anything Geoff says is worth listening to and if you have any involvement with decks you would be wise to follow the link and see what he has to say. The presentation is found at https://www.deckwood.com.au/pdf_newsletter_11_17/reliably-durable-timber-structures-tq-10-17.pd

It's a Good Idea to Pre-oil Your Decks

This month I had a call from an architect who had, very correctly, specified LifePlus oiled all round prior to installation. The builder did not read the specification (or ignored it) and so only wanted to oil the top after laying. He explained that it was going to take an extra day to oil all round. The architect stood his ground and rightly so. The builder then said, "how about I oil the underneath when it is laid." "NO! I want the oil on the surface between the deck and the joist, exactly where you cannot oil." While ever we run the risk of engaging contractors that cannot read or want to cut corners, It solves a lot

of problems if you specify your LifePlus with one coat of factory applied Tanacoat and then, just before handover give the top of the deck another coat. For more information contact Stuart Madill, Wilson Timbers 0403 385 707.

Note: Deckwood and LifePlus profiles are covered by an Australian Registered Design.

The Customer Isn't Always Right

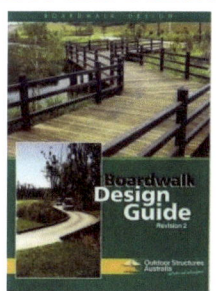 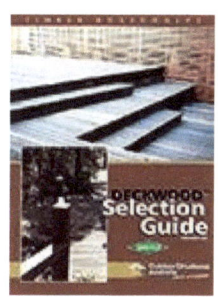 

Last week I had one of my most frustrating phone calls ever. Outdoor Structures Australia passed on to me an enquiry from a firm of engineers that were pricing a design and construct tender for a boardwalk and wanted a price on materials. Those materials were 300x75 KD joists but only spanning 4 m and 75x25 mm decking spanning 600 mm. I was quite blunt I fear. The joists are way oversize in an impossible specification (you cannot dry beyond 50 mm thick) and 75x25 mm would not pass a domestic deck load let alone a commercial one. "Why are you trying to reinvent the wheel" I asked, because everything is already sorted for you in my three guides. Two of these are available free off the net and the last is only $55. "Oh we wouldn't countenance purchasing a guide, just give me a price for the materials!" "You have not understood; the joists cannot be supplied as you have specified and the decking mustn't be supplied. " I even offered to send through some CAD drawings of systems that work. No! I just want a price and now some poor unsuspecting council may well receive something very unsuitable.

When it comes to external timber design I firmly believe that design and construct is a very poor way to progress. The design needs to be done either by specialist or by firms willing to learn, ask questions and avail themselves of the very best guides to the subject. See The City of Gold Coast Builds an Outstanding Deck in the July 2017 Newsletter Actually, it is not that hard, I was thrown out of school after grade 10.

Timber Garden Retaining Walls

WoodSolutions have released a new Design Guides, Timber Garden Retaining Walls (Number 41). A garden wall is one under 1 m high and often does not need council approval. It is a great resource, written for both design and landscaping professionals and ambitious DIY'ers.

The body of the publication is devoted to a discussion of design, materials and construction details. Useful information includes tables showing recommended spans, post depths and fixing details. These are complemented by drawings of typical construction systems, including connections, drainage, backfill and other functional elements.

Writing a Book on External Furniture

I have started to write a book on external furniture and I live in hope that the royalties from this book will allow me to purchase a genuine Eames lounge and Ottoman, a chair with "the warm, receptive look of a well-used first baseman's mitt." (In reality it probably won't finance an Aldi copy.) This iconic chair has been in constant manufacture without significant modification since 1956 because its molded plywood, heavy leather padding, adjustable height and reclining action allows it to conform to almost any body.

This very successful chair highlights the problem with external furniture. Molded plywood will disintegrate, the leather will not take the ravages of the sun and rain and overall it is far from being robust enough for commercial use. The designer of external furniture must produce, not just code compliant but also comfortable furniture without any recourse to padding, height adjustment or reclining action. And on top of that it has to last for years. This is very challenging and a seeming impossibility, hence the book.

Is it worth writing the book? Financially, no. But as Prof. Marton Marosszeky, a Director of BCRC, the construction materials and durability consultants I now work with said "I find that you learn a lot in the writing, and it builds your knowledge, so if you have the time I would go for it." I am also being encouraged by Ralph Bayley of Guymer Bailey Architects who has done some very impressive work with external furniture.

I am on the lookout for images and insights from my readers. Images I need are:
Decay under film finish.
Decayed sapwood
Failed glue joints
Badly weathered hardwood BBQ table.
Badly weathered pine BBQ table

I also want to know if you have had experience with jarrah. Any images and comments related to this new book will be greatly received.

December 2017

Another Deck Collapse
How to Confirm the Correct Treatment Has Been Achieved
The Importance of Grading Timber
Lessons From a 30 Year Old Mangrove Boardwalk

Another Deck Collapse

Just as I was about to hit send on this newsletter, the news came through about another deck collapse with yet again more fatalities and injuries. It is too early to find out why but already there are calls for annual inspections of the decks of rental properties. My report last month on a presentation by Geoff Stringer of Hyne which asks, "Should decks be load limited" is very pertinent. Here is the link. In my book *Timber Joints* I discuss decks which are usually built to the lowest price, with joints that are stressed from the weather and have no expiry date. It is a recipe for disaster if things continue the way they are. Fortunately, doing it well is not hard either. It is all in my books.

How to Confirm the Correct Treatment Has Been Achieved

This segment was mainly written by Tim Evans of IVS as a guest contributor with some tweaking from me. Not a paid advertisement

The A and B sample identified with the charge number.

The wisdom shown by Cairns Regional Council to include product testing as well as confirmation grading in the specification for the replacement decking at the esplanade has set a precedent that should be widely followed. This is necessary to ensure that the market receives correctly treated timber that will always be fit for purpose. This particular application will see the timber exposed to wave action so a higher level of protection than is normally required was needed. Readers will recall that I have been critical of the state of timber preservation coming from some suppliers, particularly with pine. Here is some articles if you missed them.

Timber Newsletters 2014-2017

July 2017 - A reminder about pine
Sept 2017 - What is needed in a wood encouragement policy

My old friend, Tim Evans, established IVS (Independent Verification Services) in Australia, five years ago but, not surprisingly, has had difficulty getting traction with Third Party Quality Assurance, with the "excuse" that it costs too much. In reality though, it will cost cents per M3 once in place. The lack of any compulsion, vis regulation/law is the game stopper. It is a given, and has been well proven by his and my own practical experience with the operation of timber preservation plants, where regular product testing, coupled with charge sheet reconciliation, not only insures compliance with AS 1604, but insures that the unnecessary cost of overtreatment is avoided. In the past, NSW & QLD had the TMA & TUMA which provided some incentive, but with the repeal of these acts it is partly cowboy country which is bad for wood.

The samples shown above that were taken in Cairns, along with others from the four charges involved., have been dispatched and logged into IVS's portal. The portal provides:

- Client's ability to register own samples for analysis to AS 1604.
- Secure data protection with individual Log On and Password.
- Data stored and backed up permanently.
- Clients with multiple sites & plants can vary levels of access on "need to know".
- Provides chain of custody.
- Purchase order & billing are linked with the portal.

Tim advised me that timber product testing has shown steady growth, and will in the next year or so be expected to show more growth with the long overdue NCBP Legislation in Queensland. This legislation is being watched with interest by other states. Tim understands that a Manager, Non-conforming Building Products Industry Quality, has been appointed. and a team of Inspectors with wide ranging powers is being appointed. If you want to know more, Tim can be contacted as follows **m 0417 726 741   p 1800 812 498   e** tim.evans@ivsltd.com.au

The Importance of Grading Timber

I am here pictured in Cairns inspecting timber produced to the Deckwood specification. I was impressed with the level of conformance. The mill did say that they had exceptional logs but at the end of the day it is about culling out non-conforming material at the mill before the timber is delivered. The last batch I graded to the same specification had a 50% non-conformance including untreated lyctus susceptible sapwood!

In the absence of industry wide checks I recommend that timber in public structures be graded independently for

conformance. I can do this, it can be organised through Timber Queensland and for our NSW readers contact Richard Forrester at Timber Inspection Ph 0429 646112.

Consider this decking which overall had about a 75% non-conformance. The mill didn't give a hoot (I could have used a much stronger word), The builder didn't give that much stronger word, and the certifier had absolutely no idea what he/she was looking at. There is no point putting effort into design if you allow this! Responsible suppliers deserve and need your protection and if you don't, what will you have left? As Tim said above, cowboy country.

Lessons from a 30-year-old mangrove boardwalk

The Jack Barnes Bi-centennial Mangrove Boardwalk is situated adjacent to the Cairns Airport and was constructed 30 years ago as a work for the dole project. It is still in service and, having walked it, I believe there are lessons to be learnt from it.

Subframe.

The piles are bamboo about 6m long which were cut off about a half a metre below the surface and a length of sewer pipe was spliced in and filled with concrete. In places they have sunk but, overall, it is functioning as at most it only has to support a handful of people. As far as supporting the normal design load of 5 kPA, 4.5 kN it would fail. The local footy club is no longer allowed to run on it as the boardwalk developed a "bow wave" action. Compare the piles to those at the Nudgee Beach boardwalk, our first big boardwalk where the piles were 2x6 m spliced H5 pine with a physical barrier against marine attack.. A special small tracked pile driver was used which worked off ply matting. When the tide came in it raised itself above the tide so it did not have to disturb the environment getting back to dry ground. Unfortunately that machine is no longer in service.

Timber

The timber is in remarkably good condition and has many years service left despite already being 30 years old. This is largely because the top surface of most boards e clear of defect. Those with defect have degraded but they are a very small minority. You cannot get this grade of timber now if you ask for F14 or F17 and that is why [Deckwood](#) was developed. You need to purchase my book on Grading Hardwood to understand why a very tight specification is required for decking.

The timber is believed to be forest red gum an In Ground Durability 1 timber. I have had mixed results with this timber. It used to be one of the permitted species for Deckwood because what we sourced from the Lockyer Valley performed very well. When we closed our mill and I started to get it from further afield there were a number of claims, mainly for "shelling out: which is a delamination of the growth rings. When I went back to the mills involved one said, "We wondered why you were using it, we could have told you it was unsuitable." The timber size is 100x50 which has a width to thickness ratio of 2 to 1 and I have observed that the chunkier sizes are less prone to shelling out. No idea why.

Despite the species obvious success here, I would advise against using it for decking as this variability works against the certainty you need when doing a design. It cost me thousands. Its use in joists is an issue now too. I have in the past used forest red gum for boardwalk joists. A good piece went F17 and as it was durability Class 1 in ground, it should d have been good. Unfortunately, its strength has been re-classified in AS2082-2007. Earlier in AS2082-2000 Forest red gum in Structural Grade 2 went F14 and Structural Grade 1, the highest grade, went F17. Now both grades only meet F14 unseasoned (AS2082 Table A3) and when dry F17 (Table A1) Spotted gum in the highest grade would be F22 and F34 respectively.

Fasteners

The fasteners and the brackets are all galvanised and this deck is fastened with galvanised flat head nails. The areas closest to the creek have experienced the most corrosion but, being 30 years old these would have been Australia made bolts which perform much better than the low cost imported bolts. See June 16 newsletter - Galvanised bolts more variable than timber. I recommend stainless steel. A detailed argument for this is given in my book Timber Joints.

The heads of the nails showed no corrosion and had not worked out which surprised me in this very demanding application. Flat head nails were available with a twisted shank which I imagine were used. Now nails are imported so I expect similar issues as with the bolts.

Maintenance

When first constructed the council would regularly blow the deck to remove litter between the deck gaps and the joist but, I am led to believe, this has not be done for a long time. A very few boards and kerbs have been replaced. Overall the costs have been very low.

Future

The foundations that are sinking in places do need some attention, probably more for aesthetics than safety but, once attended to, provided the traffic remains light the superstructure will give many years of satisfactory service.

About the Author

Ted Stubbersfield was born in the small Queensland town of Gatton in 1950. After studying to be a pastor in Brisbane and the UK he returned to the family business, Gatton Sawmilling Co. A fair question would be, can anything good come out of Gatton? Well, Gatton was the home of a Governor General of Australia (William Vanneck 1938). It is also the home of the best and most innovative hardwood producer in Australia, Outdoor Structures Australia (OSA).

The family had been involved in sawmilling and building for about 140 years and a lot of knowledge has passed through the generations. In 1985 we ventured into the footbridge market (almost by accident) and then followed public landscaping. Initially we just did as we were told by consultants who knew very little about timber. In about 1988 Ted decided he would come to know the medium he was working with far better than any of his competitors and most of the professionals who used his products.

Ted realised that there were no useful standards and guides for designing and building weather exposed timber structures such as boardwalks. That led in 1997 to his first formal research project on boardwalk design, engineering supply and construction. Over the years there followed a complete set of guides. These allowed professionals to design timber structures of exceptional beauty and durability. Typically, everybody wants to re-invent the wheel and the guides were usually ignored. Invariably, the same mistakes keep being made over and over. The newsletters in this book were an attempt to make designers aware of issues.

In 2012, the time came to close the manufacturing arm of OSA and to take on a less stressful lifestyle. Ted plans to put in writing much of what he has learnt so the industry does not have to relearn it. Readers of my timber design files will see the genesis of much of their content in these newsletters and a lot more besides. Many of these newsletters were prompted by some poor designer giving me a call with a tale of woe over a job that had gone badly. These newsletters are intended to help you avoid a similar situation.

www.ingramcontent.com/pod-product-compliance
Lightning Source LLC
Chambersburg PA
CBHW042129010526
44111CB00031B/36